Robert Baker Girdlestone

The Foundations of the Bible

Studies in Old Testament Criticism. Second Edition

Robert Baker Girdlestone

The Foundations of the Bible
Studies in Old Testament Criticism. Second Edition

ISBN/EAN: 9783337099893

Printed in Europe, USA, Canada, Australia, Japan

Cover: Foto ©Lupo / pixelio.de

More available books at **www.hansebooks.com**

THE
FOUNDATIONS OF THE BIBLE:

STUDIES IN OLD TESTAMENT CRITICISM.

BY

R. B. GIRDLESTONE, M.A.,

Hon. Canon of Christ Church ; late Principal of Wycliffe Hall, Oxford ;
Author of Old Testament Synonyms, &c.

SECOND EDITION.

EYRE AND SPOTTISWOODE,

Her Majesty's Printers :

LONDON—GREAT NEW STREET, FLEET STREET, E.C.

EDINBURGH, GLASGOW, MELBOURNE, & NEW YORK.

1891.

PREFACE.

THIS book is not intended to be an *eirenicon* between the advanced critic and the student who stands in the old paths; but it may prepare the way for some better mutual understanding by recalling both parties to a consideration of the first principles of sound Biblical criticism. An attempt, at least, is here made to set forth the literary claims of the Pentateuch and the later Historical Books of the Old Testament in the light of such critical principles as we should naturally apply to all other ancient historical literature. The result is a modification of the old view—somewhat in the direction of the new—but also a vindication of the literary fidelity of the writers, and of the substantial integrity of the Books. On the one hand, marks of compilation and of editorship, together with the use of documents, have been observed throughout; on the other, cause is shown for believing that the Law preceded the Prophets, and that we still have, in the main, the original works of Moses and those that followed after. The foundations of the Bible have thus been re-examined and proved to be historical and trustworthy.

It would be beside the purpose of such a book to follow in detail the analytical and destructive criticism which has travelled from the Continent to England, and which has been popularised by men of note occupying Professorial Chairs in our country. For such criticism of critics and discussion of *minutiæ* it will be enough to refer to Bissell's work on the Pentateuch (Clark), to Vos on the Mosaic Origin of the Pentateuchal Codes (Hodder), or to the more critical examination of the sacred text which is being carried on by Dr. Green, of Princeton, U.S. It has seemed wiser in the present enterprise to take salient points, and so to clear the path; the object being to present something positive rather than negative, and to construct rather than to criticise : to give, in fact, a view of the Sacred Books which might reassure any reader whose mind had been disturbed or perplexed by the popular accounts of biblical criticism to be found in our ordinary periodical literature.

The lines of literary evidence which have in the main satisfied the scholars of old time have been set forth afresh in the following pages, but the results of special enquiries into some comparatively untrodden departments of the subject have been added, being based on a fairly wide and long-sustained study of the books under discussion.

It may, perhaps, be asked, What has called forth such a torrent of destructive criticism on the Old Testament narratives during the past half-century ?

Is it that fresh investigations into Hebrew and cognate languages have proved Biblical Hebrew to be later than was formerly supposed ?

Is it that some old MSS. have been discovered which have tended to shake men's faith in the trustworthiness of the Sacred Books?

Is it that some ancient monuments have been brought to light which have caused men to doubt the accuracy of the history contained in the Old Testament?

No; it is none of these things. If we must go down to

the root of the matter we are compelled to affirm that—wittingly or unwittingly—critics have been influenced by a growing disinclination to regard the Bible as *unique*. They desire to associate it with the Sacred Books of the East. They wish to economise in the domain of the supernatural, to bring down all that is professedly extraordinary in the sacred records to a level with the rest of the history of mankind, to minimise the *objective* in theology and life, thus ascribing to man or to nature that which in Scripture is assigned to God. This unconscious unwillingness to let God act—this reduction of the Divine Being to an impersonal impassive Force—is to be met with in various branches of thought, and now it has infected the Biblical student, even the Christian student.

But if such principles as these are to actuate and influence the Biblical critic, the term " criticism " will become almost a bye-word, and a critic will be no longer respected as a scholar. Our business as Biblical critics is to take into consideration all the phenomena of the text, of the language, of the contents, and of their legitimate bearing on the history and literature that sprang out of them, *i.e.* on Christianity and the New Testament. Anything less than this is unscientific. Literary phenomena, for example, must not be explained away because they involve a belief in miracles, in prophecy, or in a long-projected scheme of Divine Redemption, traceable through centuries of history, and culminating in the manifestation of Christ. If the critic clearly detects what Prof. Margoliouth described at the Hull Church Congress as " unconscious co-operation on the part of the writers," together with Providential care of the books, and the guiding hand of God in the history which they contain, then he must hold fast to these things, and

b

must let materialism drift past him while he stands on the Rock of Truth.

Many of the popular difficulties about the Bible spring from the fact that different branches of the subject are confused in the mind. It is of the A B C of criticism that we should carefully distinguish between certain questions. Let us look at them for a moment.

I. There is the question of *authorship.* It is not easy to tell when or by whom a book was written unless the author gives his name, and unless the date can be gathered clearly from the contents. Moreover, after all, name and date may be forged. We need, consequently, the voucher of early tradition, if it can be secured, in order to make sure of a writer's name. But vouchers for ancient books are difficult to attain; besides, who is to vouch for the books of a later date which bear witness to the earlier? For example : the Book of Joshua testifies to the Mosaic origin of Israelite legislation; but what of the Book of Joshua? Can it be shown to have been written, say, before the time of Samuel? and are we sure of the trustworthiness of the records concerning Samuel? and so on. It is evident that in order to make sure of our ground we must begin at the very bottom, and build up step by step from the present to the past. This is the method adopted in the following pages.

II. There is the question of *compilation.* The materials from which a book is composed may be early, yet the compiler may have lived centuries later. Who shall decide in such a case where the ancient extracts begin and end, and what is the comparative value of the several parts? Here comes in the importance of the Book of Chronicles as compared with the Books of Samuel and Kings, numerous sections of the former having been borrowed from an early copy of the latter. Attention has been called in the present volume to this remarkable literary phenomenon, for it presents a precedent and a guide in determining the analogous compilation of other books.

III. There is the question of *editorial work*. This is involved in the previous one. How far had a compiler to assume the functions of a modern editor? Had he to translate? to modernise the dialect or spelling? to revise? to add notes? Besides, it is possible that he had more than one document before him. Did he in such cases blend his materials into one? or did he make a sort of patchwork from these materials? Each of these plans would be practicable, and perhaps we have specimens of both processes in the Bible. All these matters have been borne in mind by the writer of the following pages, but, after all, he honestly confesses that he must plead ignorance about many of them.

IV. There is the question of *integrity*. Granted that we have in a certain book old materials put together by a later hand, may there not be still later interpolations? and how will they affect the character of the book as a whole? We judge of the age of a book to a large extent by the use made of it, in the way of quotations or references, by later writers. But how far does a quotation from a book carry with it the certainty that the work was then just what it is now? Circumstances will alter our judgment on such a matter. When we come across what is apparently an interpolation, as in the case of part of Gen. **36**, our attention is arrested, and we ask, What is the date of the interpolation? and what inferences are we to draw concerning the date and character of the book as a whole? The case just cited is interesting, both from its rarity and because the interpolated passage, though comparatively late, is not so late as the age in which the genealogies contained in the First Book of Chronicles were prepared.

V. There is the question of the *contents.* May we trust them wholly, or only in part, or not at all? Much will depend on the authority of the writer. Had he opportunities of knowing the facts? Was he observant, honest, candid? Was he in any sense commissioned, whether from below or from above? Here comes to our aid the ancient Jewish belief that the writers of the Old Testament histories were Prophets. The truth of the contents of a book is not done away with by the fact that the work is anonymous. We accept the record as true if it bears internal marks of credibility, and all the more if we have reason to believe that the writer belonged to a responsible and trustworthy class, and that there were no literary difficulties standing in the way of his having composed the work.

Confirmatory evidence is always desirable, but we cannot expect additional vouchers for all the *minutiæ* of ancient history. If a writer can be shown to be trustworthy in the leading outlines of his work, we are prepared to trust the filling-in of his story, unless there is definite reason to the contrary. The speeches and dialogues contained in the Old Testament histories would be covered by this rule. On the contrary, the credit of an author would suffer if he were clearly found to be mistaken in some particulars of his narrative; and if he could be proved guilty of a series of deliberate misstatements, his other assertions would command but little respect. Fortunately, the books we are discussing have no such evil reputation.

It will be observed that in conducting this enquiry the writer has not sheltered himself under the authority of

Christ—though that authority cannot easily be dismissed from the mind. When I affirm that Jesus is the Christ, I assert that He is the Person whose advent was promised in the Old Testament, and I imply my belief in a series of detailed predictions or forecasts, which run through many of the books. In fact, a thread of hope may clearly be detected from Genesis onwards throughout. It narrows and yet developes as the ages pass on; and we are left at the end of the Old Testament firmly impressed with the conviction that one of the Seed of David was to be expected, and that he should not only restore the kingdom to Israel, but should be a light to lighten the Gentiles. Thus, by believing in Jesus as the Messiah, I set my seal on the Old Testament as a record of the doings and counsels of the unseen Father.

It is a moot point at the present day whether we may go beyond this, and claim the authority of Christ in support of the traditional views of the Pentateuch and the books which follow. He evidently vouches for the authority of the Scriptures as a whole, for Moses as a law-giver, for David as a Psalmist, and for the Prophets as sacred teachers and writers; but does He affirm that the Pentateuch, as He had it (*i.e.* as we have it), is the work of Moses, and that the traditional view of the other books which was current in His time was wholly true? It seemed wisest to carry on the following enquiries without discussing this grave question. At the same time the present writer does not wish to hide his conviction that the traditional view is immensely strengthened by having been tacitly accepted by Christ,—and that, both before and after his resurrection. To ignore this fact seems to be not only irreverent on the part of a Christian, but also irrational on the part of a critic.

If, however, criticism disregards the utterances of Jesus Christ altogether, and proceeds to give up the old view of the Hebrew Scriptures all along the line, assigning them, with a greater or less degree of confidence, to the period between the Captivity and the era of the Maccabees, then the foundations of our Bible, and consequently of our beliefs and hopes, would be rudely shaken.

What should we do in such a case? Should we comfort ourselves with the reflection that if the books are frauds, at any rate they are pious frauds? By no means. The student of mediæval history knows enough about pious frauds. An honest man cannot sustain his soul on pious frauds. When he strikes out of his New Testament all references to the pious frauds of the Old, and all the theology which hangs upon them, he will find but little left with which to battle against evil and to face the day of death and that which is beyond.

No; we will carry on the war with the critic's own weapons. The Maccabean hypothesis has been conjured with enough. The farce is over. There is absolutely nothing which can certainly be called Maccabean either in the contents or in the language of the Hebrew Bible. As for the contents, every English student can judge for himself. And as for the language, there is no acknowledged Maccabean Hebrew known to be in existence. We have Biblical Hebrew and we have Talmudical Hebrew. Which of these was the language of the Maccabean era? The investigations of Prof. Margoliouth supply us with the only answer at present available.* He has shown by a process of reconstruction

---

* An Essay on *The Place of Ecclesiasticus in Semitic Literature.*
(Oxford Press.)

from three versions what class of Hebrew was in vogue when the Apocryphal Book of Ecclesiasticus was written. It proves to be not the Hebrew of the Bible, but the later degraded or middle Hebrew, which grew up after the Captivity, and was the colloquial language of the Jews till the downfall of Jerusalem, and which included "the Hebrew tongue" spoken by our Lord and His Apostles. The inference is plain, and there is no rebutting evidence; thus the last shred of hope for destructive criticism, the linguistic hope, is torn away by the linguist himself.

To conclude. We may still read our Bible as in the ancient days. When it tells us of the dealings and manifestations of God in Creation, in Providence, and in History, we may still take its record as true. We may still rest upon its exceeding great and precious promises, and believe that they are "Yea and Amen in Christ." The Word of God has been tried to the uttermost, but we may still love it.

It only remains to be said that the greater part of the following pages originally appeared as a series of papers in the *Record* newspaper; but the whole has been re-examined, re-arranged, and in part re-written.

It is possible that there may be some *errata* amongst the 950 references to the Scriptures contained in the book, but pains have been taken to reduce them to a minimum. The arguments adduced will not commend themselves equally to all minds, and the author may be accused of shutting his eyes to the difficulties of his position, or of failing to appreciate the force of opposing criticism. He has not, however, wittingly passed over any critical considerations of a linguistic character which needed to be brought forward, though he has purposely abstained from enumerating imaginary objections. Each chapter is complete in itself, and produces its own evidence ; and after due deduction is made for possible bias and over-statement, it will be found that the arguments converge and are cumulative, and it is hoped conclusive.

R. B. G.

Hampstead, 1890.

CONTENTS.

———◆———

CHAPTER I.

THE QUESTION STATED.

CHAPTER II.

WHAT DO THE BOOKS SAY OF THEMSELVES? AND WHAT DO OTHERS SAY OF THEM?

CHAPTER III.

HISTORY OF WRITING FROM THE DAYS OF NEHEMIAH UPWARDS.

CHAPTER VIII.

QUOTATIONS AND REFERENCES TRACED BACK FROM THE TIMES OF THE KINGS TO THE PERIOD OF THE JUDGES.

CHAPTER IX.

THE CASE OF JOSHUA AND THE PENTATEUCH.

CHAPTER X.

NOTES INTRODUCED INTO THE EARLY BOOKS.

CHAPTER XI.

OTHER NOTES IN THE HISTORICAL BOOKS.

CHAPTER XII.

FIDELITY OF THE WRITERS AND COMPILERS.

CHAPTER XIII.

SOME PECULIARITIES IN THE STYLE OF THE WRITERS.

CHAPTER XIV.

HISTORICAL CHARACTER OF THE BOOKS.

CHAPTER XV.

CHRONOLOGICAL ELEMENT IN BIBLICAL HISTORY.

CHAPTER XVI.

THE PRIMITIVE GENEALOGIES OF ISRAEL.

CHAPTER XVII.

GENEALOGIES IN THE LATER BOOKS.

CHAPTER XXVIII.

SUMMARY AND CONCLUSION.

THE

FOUNDATIONS OF THE BIBLE.

CHAPTER I.

THE QUESTION STATED.

Christianity and literature. THE Christian Faith, whilst eminently practical in its character, is to some extent literary in its origin. A man may believe in Christ and yet be unable to read; but probably his teacher is a reader; and certainly Christians have a strong tendency to become readers. There can be little doubt that a great impetus was given to the copying trade through the issue of the books of the New Testament towards the close of the first century of our era, and that Christianity was speedily established as a literary religion; its adherents, however lowly, regarding the possession of a Gospel or some other sacred book as a very high privilege.

The Old Testament presupposed by the New. 2. But Christianity sprang out of an older Faith; and that, too, was literary. The Lord Jesus and His immediate followers were not only Israelites nationally, but they were possessors of certain sacred books which had come down to them from ancient times and were regarded as of the highest authority. "The Law," "the Law and the Prophets," "the Scriptures," "the Holy Scriptures," "the Old Testament or Covenant," "the Psalms"—these are constantly referred to as the common property and sacred

A

heritage of all Israel. They are regarded as containing Divine utterances, whether of the nature of promise or warning, history or prophecy, law or doctrine. These old books are quoted about six hundred times in the New Testament; the mission of Christ is regarded as the fulfilment, in every detail, of utterances which they contain; the teaching of Christ claims to be judged by them; and the Christian views of God, of sin, of judgment, of righteousness, and of the Incarnation, Death and Resurrection of God's Son, presuppose such a theological foundation as is laid in the Old Testament. All adherents of the Israelite or (to use the more popular word) the Jewish creed were professedly at one with the founders of the Christian Faith in this respect. However much they might differ in questions of interpretation, however distant their hearts might be from the God whom they professedly followed, however vexed and angry they might be with Jesus of Nazareth for the authority and simplicity with which He set forth the great central truths contained in the Law and the Prophets, yet the books to which He referred were indubitably the books which they held sacred. To these books they appealed when asked by Herod where the Messiah should be born, and to these they referred when challenging Nicodemus to show whether any prophet was to arise out of Nazareth.

The Jewish Bible.

3. What, then, are the books which thus appear to be the common property of Jew and Christian? and what is their value and authority?

The simple answer which comes to every Christian's lips in answer to the first question is that they are the books contained in our Old Testament. About this there is very little discussion amongst modern critics, as the evidence, though simple, is sure. The second question calls for more patient examination.

Our first business, then, is to show the grounds for affirming that the books of the Old Testament constituted the Jewish Scriptures — neither more nor less — in our

Lord's time. That our Old Testament exactly answers to the Jewish Bible at the present day any English student can find out for himself by examining a Jewish Bible, such as that published by Trübner in 5625 (1865), translated by Isaac Leeser. The title-page of this book runs thus:— "תורה נביאים וכתובים (*i.e.* the Law, the Prophets, and the Writings). The Twenty-four Books of the Holy Scriptures: carefully translated according to the Massoretic text, after the best Jewish authorities." In the Preface the translator refers to other versions, and then proceeds to explain the three-fold division of the books. The first is the Pentateuch; the second contains Joshua, Judges, Samuel, Kings, and all the prophets except Daniel; whilst the third contains Psalms, Proverbs, Job, the five Megilloth or rolls (Song of Solomon, Ruth, Lamentations, Ecclesiastes, and Esther), Daniel, Ezra, Nehemiah, and Chronicles. The reader may not at once see how these make up twenty-four books; but the twelve minor prophets are counted as one, and the five rolls were all counted as one, these small books being written or associated together so that they might not be lost or overlooked. All modern Hebrew Bibles have the same contents and arrangement.

4. It may be interesting to compare this list of the books *Melito's list.* of the Old Testament with two very ancient catalogues, one coming to us from Christian sources and one from Jewish. In the fourth book of the *Ecclesiastical History* by Eusebius (written about A.D. 325), he gives an account of a certain Melito, Bishop of Sardis, who flourished about A.D. 170. He was a learned man, and wrote various works, *e.g.* on the Passover, on the Lord's Day, on Psychology, and on Baptism. In a letter to one Onesimus, whom he calls Brother, he says, " You were desirous of having an exact statement of the Old Testament, how many in number and in what order the books were written. When, therefore, I went to the East, I accurately ascertained the books of the Old Testament, and send them to you here below."

He then gives " of Moses five books, Joshua, Judges, Ruth, four books of Kings, two of Chronicles, Psalms, Proverbs of Solomon (which is also called Wisdom), Ecclesiastes, Song of Songs, Job, Isaiah, Jeremiah, the twelve (minor) prophets, Daniel, Ezekiel, and Esdras (*i.e.* Ezra)." It will be observed that the order of the books here is more like ours than like the Jewish, and some of the lesser books are not noticed, *e.g.* Lamentations, which would be written with Jeremiah, and Nehemiah with Ezra.

Josephus' list.

5. The Jewish writer Josephus was about contemporary with St. Paul. He wrote a book "against Apion," in which, amongst other things, he contrasts the Sacred Books of the Jews with those of the Egyptians. He says (I. 8), "We have not a countless number of books, but only two-and-twenty, which are rightly accredited. Of these five are the Books of Moses, containing the Law and the history of the generations of men up to his death. From the death of Moses to that of Artaxerxes" (*i.e.* the age of Nehemiah) "the prophets who followed Moses described the things which were done during the age of each one respectively in thirteen books. The remaining four contain hymns to God and rules of life for men." He adds that "from the time of Artaxerxes until the present period all occurrences have been written down, but they are not regarded as entitled to the like credit with those which precede them, because there was no certain succession of prophets." He further observes that "the confidence we place in our own Scriptures (γράμματα) is shown by the fact that, although so many ages have passed away, no one has dared to add to them, or to take away, or to alter. In all Jews it is implanted, even from their birth, to regard them as being the instructions of God and to abide steadfastly by them, and, if it be necessary, to die gladly for them."

This passage from the controversial writings of Josephus is of importance for many reasons. It gives us the Jewish view of the authenticity, trustworthiness, authority, and inspiration of the Old Testament, and indicates the tenacity with which the people were prepared to defend the books which they so justly held to be sacred. It will be seen that Josephus enumerates twenty-two books in the Old Testament. He probably reckoned them according to the number of the letters in the Hebrew alphabet. The question has sometimes been raised whether Josephus' enumeration included the Book of Esther, but we need not discuss this.

An assembly of Jews, held at Jamnia some time after *Council of Jamnia.* the destruction of Jerusalem, reckoned the number of the Sacred Books as twenty-four, viz., five of the Law ; eight of the Prophets (Joshua, Judges, Samuel, Kings, Jeremiah, Ezekiel, Isaiah, and the Twelve); eleven other books or writings (Ruth, Psalms, Job, Proverbs, Ecclesiastes, Canticles, Lamentations, Daniel, Esther, Ezra, Chronicles).

Jerome (A.D. 380), in his celebrated *Prologus Galeatus,* *Jerome's list.* gives this as the regular traditional Jewish reckoning, viz., five Books of Moses, Joshua, Judges (with Ruth), Samuel, Kings, Isaiah, Jeremiah, Ezekiel, the Twelve, Job, Psalms, Proverbs, Ecclesiastes, Canticles, Daniel, Chronicles, Ezra (with Nehemiah), Esther.

6. It may now be taken for granted—in fact there has seldom been any serious doubt about the matter—that our Old Testament is practically the same as the collection of books which the Jews in our Lord's time held sacred. But some one will say, What about the APOCRYPHA ? This is *The Apocrypha.* certainly a perplexing question. The Apocrypha consists of various books and parts of books of uncertain date and origin, which have been incorporated, no one knows when or by whom, into the ancient Greek translation of the Old Testament commonly called the Septuagint (LXX.). It is clear that Josephus knew them and used some of them in the preparation of his " Antiquities "; it is equally certain from the passage cited above that he did not rank them as of co-ordinate authority with the Sacred Books. In this judgment he appears to be at one with the Jewish leaders

and Christian teachers of the Apostolic age. It will therefore be unnecessary for our present inquiry that we should discuss them at all.

Traditional view of the Old Testament.

7. We now revert to the second question, which will have to be discussed more at large, viz., Whence came the Jewish Sacred Books? What is their age? Who wrote them? On what authority have they been received by Jew and Christian alike? To say that they are of God is a true but an incomplete answer. They are manifestly regarded as God-breathed, or inspired in some sense, by Jew and Christian. They teach the things of God, and are imbued with His Spirit. All who believe in God at all recognise this, though they would differ exceedingly from one another in their estimate of the religious value of different books and parts of books. But whilst the spirit of the books is of God, the body is of man, and their literary position must be judged from a man's point of view. They must be dealt with as ancient Semitic literature, and may be subjected to the same class of criticism as any other ancient documents of about the same age and style, if such are to be found.

Sir Isaac Newton's view.

Perhaps the traditional belief concerning the age and authorship of the books has never been set forth more simply and sensibly than by that great layman to whom Cambridge, England, and the world owe so much—Sir Isaac Newton. In the first chapter of his work on Daniel, he starts with the finding of the Law in the age of Josiah. " This," he adds, " is the Book of the Law now extant." He traces it back to the time of Asa and Jehoshaphat, and points out that the Pentateuch was received both by the two tribes and by the ten, the Samaritan Pentateuch being a lineal descendant of the old Law. He is thus led back to the days of the undivided kingdom, and shows that the Law was recognised by David. He proceeds to examine the Pentateuch itself, and shows that it is composed of various histories, *e.g.* the History of the Creation, composed by Moses, the Book of the Generations of Adam, and the Book of the Wars of the Lord, which was begun by Moses. These, he says, were public books, and therefore not written without the authority of Moses and Joshua; and he concludes that the Prophet Samuel had leisure, in the reign of Saul, to put them into the form of the Books of Moses and Joshua, now extant, inserting into the Book of Genesis the genealogy of the kings of Edom, until there reigned a king in Israel (Gen. **36.** 31). The Book of the Judges, he continues, was compiled after the death of Sampson out of the Acts of the Judges,— also by Samuel, who had full authority for the work. The same was the case, he considers, with the Book of Ruth. The rest of the Historical Books were brought into their present form by Ezra and Nehemiah, who had in their hands the materials left by contemporary writers.

This view is in general agreement with such a work as Graves on the Pentateuch, which our fathers regarded as almost a classic on the subject. It makes due allowance for compilation and for editorial revision; and it sufficiently recognises both the human and the divine side of these ancient compositions. Now, however, the whole question is reopened.

8. The critical inquiry into the age, authorship, and com- *Modern* pilation of the books of the Old Testament has occupied *criticism.* some minds for a considerable period, and though no finality or agreement has been reached by critical students there is a decided "tendency" in the minds of many in a certain direction. Some critics, *e.g.* Kuenen and Welhausen, have propounded very extreme views, totally antagonistic to old-fashioned notions about the Mosaic authorship of the Pentateuch, a work which they regard as having been elaborated by many hands and completed subsequent to the Captivity. Others, notably the venerable Dr. Delitzsch,* though far more moderate, are drifting slowly from their old moorings; whilst there are not wanting men in our own country of such

---

* This lover of sacred truth and friend of Israel has passed away since these pages were written.

weight and learning as the Dean of Canterbury and Professor Stanley Leathes, whose published utterances indicate
that they see no reason to depart in the main from the
traditional and *primâ facie* view of the age and authorship
of the books as a whole.

Proposed
method of
discussion.

9. It is quite clear that Christian students are not all of
one mind on the matter. It is also clear that there is no
one definite view of the books which can be set up as " the
assured result of criticism." The way is still open; it is
still possible for the student to return to the old path, if
truth demands it. We propose in the following chapters
to investigate the matter afresh, as fully as circumstances
permit, from a literary and critical point of view, and to ask
ourselves as we go along, What does the truth demand?

In undertaking such a work we have two possible courses
before us. We may take the ultra-sceptical position that
nothing is to be accepted which cannot be proved; that
every difference is a discrepancy; that prophecy and miracles are equally impossible, and brand the books which contain them as myths; that selfish motives animated the
writers; and that literature generally is to be brought down
as low (morally and chronologically) as possible. Or we
may adopt the charitable and rational hypothesis that the
writers of a series of religious books, which have come to us
on the highest authority, are to be trusted; that their words
call for a careful and not unfavourable construction; that
the historical and literary foundations on which they stand
should be fully estimated apart from the question of their
supernatural contents; that their language and contents
should nevertheless be studied together; and that linguistic
and literary difficulties should be viewed in the light of the
age and circumstances of the writers. This last is the line
which we propose to take; at the same time we must hide
nothing which appears to have a real bearing on the great
questions at issue, even though it seem to militate against
the view to which we are inclined to assent.

It is no light matter to open this subject in a popular way, and to raise questions which may seem to some almost a profanation. Critical points, involving sometimes references to the Hebrew language, will have to be brought in some intelligible way before English readers; and, whilst each chapter will aim at a certain completeness, the force of none can be fully estimated till the whole discussion is over. The attempt will doubtless be regarded by some as unwise, and by others as vain; but it has been made in the interest of English Bible students, who need help and guidance in this difficult matter, and many of whom have neither the time nor the will to read abstruse books. It will be impossible to go over the whole Old Testament. The books mainly dealt with will be the Pentateuch and the Historical Books, which constitute the backbone of the Jewish Scriptures, and which give glimpses of the origin, history, and purpose of that nation of whom Christ came according to the flesh.

CHAPTER II.

WHAT DO THE BOOKS SAY OF THEMSELVES? AND WHAT DO OTHERS SAY OF THEM?

Limits of the discussion.

1. The books which we propose to discuss are the Pentateuch, Joshua, Judges, Samuel, Kings, Chronicles, Ezra, and Nehemiah. Others may occasionally be referred to for illustration, but those now named will occupy us sufficiently. There are many problems to be dealt with when we subject a single ancient book to what is called "higher criticism," and after all has been said that can fairly be advanced we shall have to confess our hopeless ignorance on many questions; still we hope to find our way to a position which is trustworthy and secure, if not absolutely impregnable; and we will never let go our hold of what we know because there are a great many things which we do not know.

The first question.

Our first inquiry is this, What do the books say of themselves? This is always the right question to start with when examining any literary production. Other questions follow, *e.g.* What do other authorities say of these books? Afterwards we have to ask, How far do the contents and language of the books fall in with the answers given to these two questions?

Personality of the historians kept out of sight.

2. We open our Bible for the answer to our first question, and we confess to a feeling of disappointment at finding that the books at first sight say next to nothing about themselves. Genesis has not a word of preface or postscript as to its author. There is not the slightest indication in it that it is the work of Moses. The other four books of the Pentateuch, though full of narratives about Moses, and containing several references to writing which we shall have to discuss later, do not in so many words claim Moses as their author. Nor is Joshua

spoken of as the writer of the book which bears his name.
There is not a word to indicate that any one person was the
writer or compiler of the Book of Judges. The same is the
case with Samuel, Kings, and Chronicles. In all these books
the writer, if he introduces himself at all, speaks of himself
in the third person. Moreover, though a large proportion
of the materials used in these books bears the mark, or at
least has the appearance, of being more or less contemporary
with the events recorded, the writer hardly ever associates
himself with the rest of the people spoken of by using the
first person plural. We do, indeed, find this in Josh. 5. 1,
where we read that "the kings of the Canaanites heard that
the Lord had dried up the waters of Jordan until *we* were
passed over." The verse startles us as we read it from the
very rarity of an expression which to any Englishman would
be the most ordinary one to use. The style of the books, or
the genius of the language, or some peculiar feeling in the
mind of the writers evidently led them to use the third
person singular or plural, even though they themselves
might be the chief actors or participators in the events
recorded. It reminds us of the talk of childhood. Years
sometimes pass away before children get rid of the habit of
talking of themselves in the third person.

Other ancient writings may be found to exhibit this
remarkable phenomenon in style; and the Gospels themselves illustrate the same thing, being all anonymous, and
almost wholly devoid of the use of the first person, except
in conversations. No argument can be drawn from it concerning authorship. It cannot be affirmed, *e.g.* that Moses
wrote none of the Pentateuch because he is only spoken of
in the third person.

3. But we have yet to deal with the Books of Ezra and
Nehemiah. The Book of Ezra consists of two parts, the
first six chapters referring to things which happened sixty
years before the later record. There is no preface or postscript to the book to indicate its author. In the seventh

Books of Ezra and Nehemiah.

chapter, however, Ezra is introduced in the third person, and an account of his lineage and early proceedings is given; but in the twenty-seventh verse he breaks out into praise and drops the third person, saying, "Blessed be the Lord God of our fathers, who hath extended mercy unto *me*," &c. The first person runs on through the eighth and ninth chapters, but the third person is reverted to in the tenth, though there is no break in the narrative. Thus we have what may be called in modern fashion "a new departure," though it is introduced with some degree of hesitation.

How does the case stand with Nehemiah? Here, for the first time, we have a preliminary line which seems to denote the author of the book. It runs thus:—"The words of Nehemiah the son of Hachaliah." The book runs in the first person throughout, except, of course, where lists and extracts are given. It is Nehemiah's record of his own words and deeds. If the title were translated "the deeds of Nehemiah" instead of "the words," this would not interfere with the conclusion that at last we have got what we have searched for in vain all through the Biblical histories—a book the greater part of which is confessedly written by one man, who writes in the first person and gives his name.

Contrast with the Prophetic Books.

4. It is interesting to compare the historical writings with the prophetic in this matter. It seems to have been thought far more necessary to prefix the names in the latter case than in the former. Consequently all the Prophets give their names in the first verse of their writings. The Book of Daniel is partly historical and partly prophetical. Daniel is introduced in the third person in the historical part, and in the first person in the prophetical part. It remained for Nehemiah, the contemporary of Malachi, to put his name on the close of the Historical Books of the Old Testament.

Verdict of the New Testament on the Old.

5. Before critically examining the books themselves, it will be well, in the second place, to ask what ancient

tradition and external authority say on the question of the
authorship of the books under discussion. For this purpose
we turn in the first place to the New Testament, which we
here refer to not as an inspired book, but as a collection of
ancient Jewish literature of high character.

In the New Testament we find the general division of the
Hebrew Scriptures into the Law, the Prophets, and the
Psalms; answering to the ordinary Jewish arrangement of
the Law, the Prophets, and the "Writings," of which last
the Psalms constituted the first and most important part.
The passage in St. Luke to which we specially refer (24. 44)
is an important one. The risen Lord is here represented
as addressing His personal followers, and is recurring to
His former teaching. He says:—"These are the words
which I spake unto you, while I was yet with you, that all
things must be fulfilled, which were written in the law of
Moses, and in the prophets, and in the Psalms, concerning Me." The Lord thus manifestly appeals to the Old
Testament as containing Messianic hints and prophecies
which must necessarily be fulfilled; the necessity lying in
the authority of the books, which were in some sense from
God.

Nothing is here said of the authorship of the greater part
of the Old Testament, but David is elsewhere quoted as the
writer of certain Psalms, *e.g.* the second (Acts 4. 25), the
sixteenth (Acts 2. 25), and the 110th (Acts 2. 34); whilst
the names of the prophets are occasionally given, *e.g.* Isaiah
(Acts 8. 28), and Joel (Acts 2. 16). The names of the
prophetic writers or compilers of the Historical Books are
nowhere mentioned.

The case, however, is different in regard to the authorship
of the Pentateuch. Great stress is laid upon the position of
Moses. His name is freely used—not, indeed, as having
written Genesis, or even the Pentateuch as a whole, but as
leader, legislator, writer. "The Law was given by Moses"
(John 1. 17). "Did not Moses give you the Law?" (7. 19).
"Moses wrote of Me" (5. 46).

Christ and Moses.

If a tradition were already existing in the time of Christ that the Pentateuch as a whole claimed Moses as writer, compiler, or authorizer, our Lord's words did not run counter to it, but rather tended to stamp it with renewed authority. Three classes of passages illustrate this point more clearly. The Pentateuch may be divided into the historical part, the legislative, and the pre-Mosaic. The first would include the account of the burning bush. This is quoted by our Lord as from "the Book of Moses" (Mark **12. 26**). The second would include the rule concerning divorce. This is definitely stated by our Lord to be a precept written by Moses (Mark **10. 5**). The third would include the ordinance of circumcision, of which our Lord says (John **7. 22**), "Moses gave you circumcision, not that it was of Moses, but of the fathers" (*i.e.* the Patriarchs). Thus there can hardly be any serious doubt that Moses was spoken of and regarded by Christ as answerable in some sense for the substance of the Law as we have it now, and that Genesis is taken as a faithful record of the Patriarchal age.

Jewish view.

6. The Jews in our Lord's time assigned the Pentateuch unhesitatingly to Moses. This is shown by the testimony of Josephus, in a passage already cited; it is affirmed in the Talmud (*e.g.* in Baba Bathra, *circ.* A.D. 500; compare also the opening sentences of *Pirke Aboth*, the most ancient of Talmudical Treatises, which is to be found in every Jewish Prayer Book). The same belief is implied by such Jewish utterances as we find in Matt. **19. 7**; Mark **10. 3**; John **1. 45**; **7. 19**; Acts **6. 14**. It must be acknowledged, moreover, that the Scribes of that age were not critics in the modern sense, and were generally more inclined to conserve than to invent. There were parties amongst them who would keep a strict watch over one another, some being very jealous over the written Law, and others holding an oral interpretation of it to be of almost equal value. It certainly never seems to have occurred to anyone in those days that the Pentateuch was not the work of Moses.

7. But let us get back to an earlier period. How did the *Maccabean view.* matter stand in the days of the MACCABEES, who were in power 150 years further back? We find that there was the same certainty about the Prophets, the same reticence about the names of the prophetico-historic writers, the same belief about Moses. The books are freely used as true and authoritative. The names of the great men from Abraham to Daniel were in men's mouths (see 1 Mac. **2.** 52–60); "the holy books of the Scripture" were their comfort (1 Mac. **12.** 9); copies of the Book of the Law were not rare (1 Mac. **1.** 56, 57); the Law in all its leading parts was recognized as "of Moses" (1 Esdr. **1.** 6, 11; **5.** 49; Tobit **7.** 13; Ecclus. **24.** 23; Baruch **1.** 20; 2 Mac. **1.** 29; **7.** 30), and the celebrated "Song of Moses" is quoted *verbatim* as his (2 Mac. **7.** 6).

8. One of the most interesting of the Apocryphal Books is *Testimony of Ecclesiasticus.* Ecclesiasticus, which must have been composed some time (perhaps a century) before the Books of the Maccabees. Let anyone read chapters **44–49**, and note what is said of Adam, Enoch, Noah, Abraham, Isaac, Jacob, the twelve tribes, Moses, Aaron, Joshua, Caleb, the Judges, Samuel, Nathan, David, Solomon, Elijah, Elisha, Hezekiah, Josiah, Jeremiah, Ezekiel, the twelve prophets, Zorobabel, Nehemiah. Let him ask himself, What was the Bible in the writer's days? Did it not contain the Historical Books with which we have to do? Was it not substantially the same as our Old Testament?

There is not an atom of ground for the supposition that any of the books or parts of books which constitute our Old Testament were the work of men of that age. The contrary is the case. It is very noticeable that in the Preface to the Book of Ecclesiasticus by the original writer's grandson we have the identical division into the Law, the Prophets, and the other Books, which we have already seen to have been the ordinary division of the Old Testament in later days.

The words are as follows :—" Whereas many and great things have been delivered unto us by the Law and the Prophets, and by others that have followed in their steps . . . my grandfather Jesus having given himself much to the reading of the Law and the Prophets, and the other ancestral books (τῶν ἄλλων πατρίων βιβλίων) . . . not only these things, but the Law itself, and the Prophecies, and the rest of the books have no small difference (or excellence) when read in their own language." There can be very little doubt that the grouping thrice repeated in this brief preface testifies to the completeness of the Old Testament scriptures, as the Law, the Prophets, and the Writings, forming a sacred Hebrew canon in those early days.

Early traditions concerning Nehemiah and Ezra. 9. Before going farther back we must not forget the celebrated passage about Nehemiah in 2 Mac. 2. 13. This second Book of the Maccabees is professedly compiled in part from a historical work of Jason, of Cyrene, but it opens with various traditional statements of doubtful origin, some of which, he tells us, " were reported in the writings and commentaries of Neemias, who founded a library, gathering together the Acts of the Kings, and the Prophets, and of David, and the Epistles of the Kings (*i.e.* Cyrus, &c.) concerning the holy gifts." This tradition—itself recorded perhaps B.C. 150—points to the then existing belief that Nehemiah put together the Sacred Writings which now constitute the Old Testament. The Law of Moses, indeed, is not specified, possibly because that was universally known and its origin taken for granted. How far this tradition is true, and if so, on what principles Nehemiah proceeded in arranging the library or collection of Sacred Books, we cannot certainly tell. Another Jewish tradition points to Ezra rather than Nehemiah as the chief collector or editor of the O. T., and attributes a prophetic character to him. (*See* Eusebius' quotation of Irenæus, Church History, v. 8.)

The traditional view rational. These two, Ezra and Nehemiah, were men of high position, one of the tribe of Levi, and the other possibly of

Judah; one a ready scribe, the other a Pasha. They were both
men of piety and prayer, and were associated for the purpose
of actively promoting the spiritual welfare of Israel at the
close of the Old Testament period. They both clearly saw the
moral dangers and difficulties which beset the people, and
the culpable weakness of the priestly order; they both felt
themselves to be under the special guidance and influence of
the Spirit of God, and were acknowledged afterwards as
prophets. Nothing seems more reasonable, from a literary
as well as from a religious point of view, than that in their
time the books which had been preserved and regarded as
sacred in bygone ages should be brought together, and that
arrangements should be made for their safe keeping in time
to come.

Of course this is only a theory, but it fits fairly with the
facts all round; if any one has a better theory to propose he
must see how it fits all the facts. Even if this hypothesis
is accepted, it manifestly leaves a great deal of room for the
modification and compilation of documents before Nehemiah's
time, but hardly for the incorporation of other considerable
documents afterwards, for this would not lightly be permitted in such a class of literature and with people of such
a character as the Jews.

10. Of one thing we may be quite certain; nothing would
be introduced into the "Sacred Library" which was not be-
lieved to be "prophetic," and therefore in some sense Divine, *The writers of the Old Testament prophetic.*
and although there were occasionally men after Nehemiah's
time who had semi-prophetic gifts, the Jews do not acknowledge them as prophets in the full sense of the word. This
may be illustrated by three well-known passages in the First
Book of Maccabees. In chap. 4. 46 we are told that in the
days of Judas Maccabæus the defiled stones of the altar were
laid up in a convenient place "until there should come a
prophet to show what should be done with them." In
chap. 9. 27 we read that "there was great affliction in
Israel, the like whereof was not since the time that a

B

prophet was not seen among them." And in chap. **14.** 41 we are told that the Jews and priests were "well pleased that Simon should be their governor and high priest for ever, until there should arise a faithful prophet." The second of these passages puts the prophets in the far past, whilst the first and last give a prospect that prophets might arise in the future (with a possible reference to such a passage as Deut. **18.** 15); but all three imply that the Maccabæan priest-kings, though heroes and patriots raised up by God, were not regarded as prophetic men. If *they* were not prophets, who were? We look in vain down the remains and traditions of Hebrew history between the age of Nehemiah and the Christian era for the appearance of any men who would venture to add to or take from the Sacred Library or Canon which existed in Nehemiah's days.

Summary.　　11. Thus far we have seen, first, that only the two latest authors of the Historical Books write in the first person, and give their names; secondly, that there is a consensus of Jewish and Christian testimony leading to the conclusion that the Canon of the Old Testament was practically closed in the age of Nehemiah; thirdly, that the Pentateuch was thenceforward regarded as the work of Moses, and the Historical Books as the work of prophetic men, about whose names we are left in the dark.

The case of the Old Testament is in this and many other respects analogous with that of the New. The one was the work of Moses and the prophets; the other was from the hands of Apostles and prophets; and the prophetic office was regarded as carrying with it a certain authority and commission to write and a certain inspiration which would make the writings profitable for future ages.

CHAPTER III.

HISTORY OF THE ART OF WRITING, FROM THE DAYS
OF NEHEMIAH UPWARDS.

1. We have now traced the Old Testament back to the *Writing in the age of Nehemiah.* days of Nehemiah (400 B.C.); but there is a period of about a thousand years between his age and that of Moses; yet Moses is claimed as the writer of some of the scriptures which Nehemiah possessed. If it could be shown that the art of writing was not known in Moses' days, his claim would fare badly indeed. Our next business must therefore be to trace the history of writing upwards from the last books of the Old Testament, and see where we are landed; we must then look elsewhere for confirmation of our position.

Writing was common enough in the days of Nehemiah. We find him in the seventh chapter of his book and the fifth verse referring to "a register of the genealogy of them which came up at the first," *i.e.* in the days of Zorobabel. The word here translated register is the old סֵפֶר (*sepher*), and means a book, but the word translated register in the 64th verse means "writing" (כְּתָב), as in Ezra 2. 62. Neither of these words denotes the shape of the book or the material of which it was composed. The word here translated "genealogy" (יַחַשׂ) is quite peculiar, being one of a list of words only to be found in Chronicles, Ezra, and Nehemiah, and tending to show that these books are about coeval. It is always translated in the same way, so that the English student can trace its usage with a concordance, and he will be led to the conclusion that almost every family in Israel had its written archives or family papers. In other words, they were a literary people.

In Nehemiah 8 we find reference to another class of

literature. Ezra "the scribe" brings out "the book of the law of Moses," and it is read from morning light till midday. The next day the reading is continued, and brings the hearers on to Leviticus **23**, where they found written that they should dwell in booths. The reading is pursued for several days from "the book of the law of God," which must evidently have been a considerable volume.

The form of books. 2. It may be observed in passing that this book is said to have been "opened" (verse 5), not "unrolled," so that it was possibly book-shaped. In later days the Pentateuch was always written as a roll. It is much more easy to introduce notes or alterations into a book than into a roll, and when once the roll form was adopted the text would be practically fixed. The Book of Isaiah is said to have been folded up, and unfolded in the days of our Lord, the Greek word (πτύσσω) being used of folding tablets or books rather than rolls. We cannot, however, lay stress on the words used in either of these cases, as they may have been the ordinary Jewish terms for opening or unrolling any kind of document. Probably the Ethiopian eunuch's copy of Isaiah was in the form of a book.

Sealing. There was more reading in the Book of the Law in Neh. **9**. 8, and at the end of the chapter there is a covenant written and made sure (the Hebrew idioms are quite peculiar), and a considerable number of leading men put their seal to it, the seal being engraved with the name, like one found in Jerusalem by the Palestine explorers with the name of Haggai on it.

The system of engraving names on seal-rings is very ancient indeed. It may be traced back in the Bible to the time of Moses and Aaron, if not to the time of Joseph, who wore Pharaoh's ring (Gen. **41**. 42). The word for a ring is always the same, and is supposed to be Egyptian, while the word for a seal is a true Semitic one. There is a peculiar term used for the engraving of signets all through the Old Testament, from Exod. **28**. 9 and onwards. It is now considered an Egyptian word, or at any rate of Egyptian origin, though it has assumed the form of the verb פָּתַח, which simply means "to open."

3. There are frequent references in the Book of Ezra to writings, such as proclamations, genealogies, decrees, letters, copies, rolls, commissions. There are three different words translated "letter" in the book; also quite a peculiar word, translated "copy," found nowhere else but in Esther, and then spelt differently. In chap. 6. 1 and 2 we read that there was found at Achmetha (Ecbatana) "a roll in the house of the rolls, containing a record thus written," &c. Here is a *Megillah* (roll) in the house of *Sepharim* (books) containing a memoir or memorandum on which a decree is subsequently based. These books may have been tablets or cylinders, or they may have been papyrus or parchment scrolls; probably they were of different kinds. Thanks to the patience and ingenuity of explorers and decipherers, we know a good deal now about the special places in which books were stored up in the old Oriental cities. Many ancient records have perished, but those made of baked clay have to a large extent survived. *References to writing in Ezra.*

The word translated "scribe" in Ezra and elsewhere is always the same, and is to be found all through the Old Testament from Judges 5. 14 onward, being the same root as the word translated "book" (*sepher*) in Genesis 5. 1, &c. The verb means to recount or reckon rather than to write, and the scribe might be clerk, copyist, accountant, registrar, or any other literary official. Ezra himself was a "ready scribe in the law of Moses" (7. 6), and "a scribe of the words of the commandments of the Lord and of His statutes to Israel" (verse 11). *Scribes.*

4. We now take a step further back, to the period of the Captivity, which may be conveniently illustrated from the prophets Jeremiah and Ezekiel. We read of Jeremiah dictating whilst Baruch his scribe writes "with ink in the book" (Jer. 36. 18). This book is in the form of a roll *The age of Jeremiah.*

(*Megillah*), and the "leaves" (verse 23) are the columns (literally, "doors") in which the writing of rolls is usually arranged, as may be seen in any Hebrew MS. of the Pentateuch or the Book of Esther. The prophet Ezekiel (chap. 4. 1) is told to take a tile or brick (לבנה) and lay it before him and portray (lit., engrave) on it a plan of the city. This would be done with a graving-tool, and the brick would be subsequently burnt.

The age of Hezekiah.
Earlier, in Isaiah's time (chap. 8. 1), we read of the writing on a great roll, or cylinder, or tablet with a man's pen, or, rather, graving-tool (חרט); the prophet is also directed to take a tablet (chap. 30. 8) and a book, in which certain things were to be noted (lit., decreed or engraved, חקק) for the time to come, or, rather, as it is in the margin, for the latter day. The letter which Hezekiah spread before the Lord was probably written on papyrus. The Hebrew word for this letter is simply *sepher*, and the same is used of Merodach-baladan's letter (comp. Isa. 37. 14, and 39. 1). We may gather from these passages that the writers of Hezekiah's age were familiar with two classes of writing, that which was effected with a reed on paper and skin, and that which was produced with a graving-tool on unbaked clay, whether in the cylinder or tablet form.

The period of the Judges.
5. There are plenty of references to books and letters in earlier times, and to shorten our inquiry we may now go back as far as Judges 5. 14, where we read that the tribe of Zebulun contained them that handle the pen of the writer, whilst in chap. 8. 14 one of the young men of Succoth is said to have written down (A. V. "described") the names of seventy-seven headmen of the village. Writing was evidently not a rare gift in those days. It is true that the Revisers have altered the first of these passages, and read "out of Machir came down governors, and out of Zebulun they that handle the marshal's staff." But the word translated governor properly signifies an engraver (חקק); "staff" is better than "pen," but "marshal" is a vague word. The

Hebrew is *Sopher*, which we have already referred to as signifying "scribe" or "registrar," and which sets forth some literary office. The scribe's staff of office may have been of the kind familiar to Egyptologists.

We now step back into what is professedly an earlier *The age of* state of things, namely to the old boundary lists which were *Joshua.* written down in the days of Joshua. It was no easy task which was to be performed, but picked men were selected from certain tribes, "and they went and passed through the land and described it (lit., wrote it) by cities into seven parts in a book" (Josh. **18**. 9). Where such a survey was possible, literary powers were surely not in their infancy.

6. Another backward step brings us to the age of Moses. In *The age of* his extreme old age he is instructed to write the song which *Moses.* all Israel was to learn, Deut. **31**. 19; but the Book of the Law had been previously written (Deut. **29**. 27 ; **30**. 10 ; **31**. 9).

The journeyings of Israel through the wilderness were written by Divine command (Num. **33**. 2). We are also told that lists of officials were written down (Num. **1**. 17 and **11**. 26). In the first of these passages the word translated "expressed" might be rendered "notched" or "pierced," and refers to some particular method of obtaining the names, possibly similar to that in which the sheriffs are "pricked" by the Queen. This word (נָקַב) is also used in Gen. **30**. 28 ("*appoint* me thy wages"), and in some of the later books of the Bible, having been retained as an old idiom (see 1 Chron. **12**. 31 ; Ezra **8**. 20; Amos **6**. 1). The pedigrees named at the period of the Exodus were probably written documents, as in later days, though the word for "genealogy," which we found so freely used in Chronicles, Ezra, and Nehemiah, is conspicuous by its absence where we should naturally expect it, in Num. **1**. 18. This is one of many instances of the linguistic accuracy of the Biblical writers, to which attention will be directed later on.

We thus get back to the first distinct mention of writing in the Bible, viz., Exod. **17**. 14, where, after describing the war with the Amalekites, we are told that the Lord said unto Moses, "Write this for a memorial in a book (or *the* book), and rehearse it in the ears of Joshua." Thus it was both to be written in the itinerary which would already have been commenced, and was to be rehearsed orally, so as never to be forgotten. Compare the later references to this particular incident in Deut. 25. 17 and 1 Sam. 15. 2, both of which passages presuppose the narrative preserved in Exodus.

The Shote-rim. 7. There is a word used twenty-five times in the Hebrew Bible, and translated officer, ruler, or overseer. It is found as late as the Chronicles and as early as Exod. 5. 6. This word *shoter* (שֹׁטֵר) is almost always translated in the LXX. by the ordinary word for a scribe (γραμματεύς). Gesenius considers that it means to cut, as with a sword, then to inscribe, and then to order or superintend. Those who are familiar with the walls of ancient Egyptian temples and tombs will remember the frequent appearance of the scribe taking notes of all the things being done, *e.g.* the tale or tally of the bricks, and will understand how easily an inscribing-tool might become the symbol of an official. The root of the word is Semitic, and is found in Arabic and Syriac, and is apparently not traceable to an Egyptian origin. Too much stress must not be laid upon this word, but it may be taken along with the other indications in the Book of Exodus as indicating that the Israelites were not quite such an illiterate people as some have supposed.

Antiquity of the art of writing. 8. We have now traced the history of writing back from the days of Nehemiah to the age of Moses, some fourteen or fifteen centuries before the Christian era. We proceed to ask whether there is any inherent impossibility in the points elicited. It might have been thought so once. There have been times when the art of writing would be regarded as unknown in the days of Moses, or even of Joshua and the Judges, but we know better now.

If we look at Egyptian literature, the matter becomes *In Egypt.* clear. We have not only the semi-religious and semi-biographical inscriptions on the walls of the temples and tombs and on the obelisks of Egypt, but we have papyrus rolls of an exceedingly early date. It has been thought that there are indications of alphabetical writing as early as the time of the Patriarchs; at any rate, there are in the British Museum papyrus documents which have come down from that age, so that if it had happened that writing should have been referred to as in use in the days of Abraham, there would have been nothing in such a statement to shake our faith in the trustworthiness of the book which contained it. In truth, there is considerable reason to suppose that there were such documents, both genealogical and biographical: see, for example, the opening words of Gen. 5. 1— "This is the book of the generations of Adam." Nor need one hesitate to come to the conclusion that some system of writing on clay, rock, or other less durable substance came into existence in a very early stage of human history, being probably about coeval with the dispersion of the families of the human race.

Putting aside all reference to the Hittite inscriptions, *In Mesopotamia.* there have been brought to light in Mesopotamia complete libraries of books, lists, treatises, contracts, and other documents which take us back towards the period of the Judges; and before them we get back to the old Babylonian empire and the Accadian inscriptions, some of which are far older than the days of Moses, and take us back to the age of Abraham.

Professor Sayce tells us that an Assyrian library was established at Calah about 1300 B.C., but he points out that their learning was borrowed from Babylon, and that the oldest Babylonian literature is translated from Accadian, the knowledge of which was kept up by the learned in those ancient times long after it had become practically dead. Certainly these Accadians were a wonderful people. "They were the earliest civilizers of Western Asia; to them the arts and sciences, the philosophy, and many of the religious traditions not only of the Babylonians and Assyrians, but also of the Phœnicians and Syrians, have to be traced; from them the germs of Greek art and a great part of the Greek pantheon and mythology originally came; both Jerusalem and Athens were profoundly influenced by their ideas; and much of our present culture had its first starting-point in primæval Accad." (Sayce's *Assyrian Life and History*, p. 50.)

The celebrated Deluge Tablets claim to be an Assyrian translation of part of an Accadian epic in twelve books, arranged according to the signs of the Zodiac, and dating from more than 2000 B.C. " Like most epics (says Professor Sayce), it was probably of slow growth, and in its final form was pieced together out of earlier materials; and for the first origin of the lays we must go back to a past already half-forgotten in the days of Abraham."

Summary.

9. We need not determine dates, but leave these facts to speak for themselves, being content with the conclusion already arrived at, viz., that from the Exodus and onwards there were writers as well as readers amongst the Israelites, as amongst their neighbours east and west, and that there is no reason, so far as the history of writing is concerned, why Moses should not be regarded as having committed in writing to his successors such a body of literature as we possess in the Pentateuch. It then becomes simply a question of evidence, or if evidence fails us when dealing with matters of such exceeding antiquity, we must be content with the balance of probabilities, in which must be included linguistic and other considerations.

CHAPTER IV.

1. The last chapter has cleared the way for further discussion. We are evidently in a literary age all the way back from Nehemiah to Moses, and we may proceed to examine the books with care. It is evident that a considerable portion of them were compiled from older sources. This is manifestly the case with the history of the kingly period, to which we must confine ourselves in the present chapter.

The series of historical documents referred to during this *Materials for David's history.* period commences with the age of DAVID, nothing being reported as to previous annals. We are told (1 Chron. **29. 29**) that "the acts of David the king, first and last, . . . are written in the book of Samuel the seer, and in the book of Nathan the prophet, and in the book of Gad the seer, with all his reign and his might, and the times that went over him, and over Israel, and over all the kingdoms of the countries." There are many things in this passage which call for our attention. The Book of Chronicles is generally acknowledged to be comparatively late, and it gives only a selection of historical events, some of which agree almost word for word with the accounts in Samuel and Kings, whilst the rest must have been obtained from other sources. Do the three books enumerated above contain all the historical materials from which the chronicler composed his history of David's times? This seems highly probable. Were they still extant in the chronicler's time? Apparently they were. Are they included, partially or wholly, in our Books of Samuel and Kings, or were they official acts and documents of a semi-secular character? This is not so easily answered.

It seems clear that the three books were all of the same stamp, being all described by the term דברים (A.V. book), which literally means "words," but which stands for a record of deeds or "transactions," and so is rightly rendered *history* in the margin, whilst at the beginning of our verse it is translated *acts*. Now were these three writers, Samuel, Nathan, and Gad, in a position to contribute three consecutive sections to a contemporary record of David's life? Certainly they were. Samuel the seer could contribute the early chapter concerning the anointing. Gad the prophet could tell about the period of persecution, for we find him in communication with David at the very time (see 1 Sam. 22. 5). He comes again on the scene in 2 Sam. 24. 11, where he is described as "the prophet Gad, David's seer," and is apparently adviser, monitor, and almost private chaplain to the king. He also assisted David, in conjunction with Nathan, in arranging the musical services of the Temple (2 Chron. 29. 25). The third contributor is Nathan, who is called, not seer (ראה), but visionary (חזה). He appears later in the history than Gad. It was after David had fought his battles that he tells Nathan his feeling about building a House for God. Guided by a vision in the night, Nathan stays his hand, and at the same time utters the great promise which is the true basis of all Messianic prophecy (2 Sam. 7. 4–16). Nathan's next recorded mission to David was in connection with Bathsheba; and it is interesting that one of Bathsheba's children was named Nathan, and that our Lord sprang really not from Solomon but from the namesake of the prophet. We need not pursue Nathan's history further; he outlived David; and we can readily see that he, in conjunction with the other two prophets, was of all men the most suitable to contribute chapters to the history of David.

Recorders and official writers.

2. These men were not, however, official recorders. If we turn to 2 Sam. 8. 16, 17, and 1 Chron. 18. 15, we find that Jehoshaphat, the son of Ahilud, was the recorder, and

Seraiah (or Shavsha) was the scribe. In the margin we find the recorder called a remembrancer, *i.e.* a writer of chronicles. The recording may also include the writing or registering of David's own compositions (see 1 Chron. **16.** 4). Thus there may have been both sacred and secular recorders and scribes. The administration of the kingdom in David's days was very complete, and there must have been something answering to our Home Office, with an army of clerks in it, to carry out the system so methodically described in the First Book of Chronicles.

If any student will take the trouble to compare the history of David's times as given in Chronicles with that given in Samuel and Kings, he will find that, putting aside genealogical and other official lists, the chronicler could have found all his materials in an early recension of Samuel and Kings, with the exception of some sections which seem to be traceable to certain officials, such as Samuel's grandson Heman, and his partners, Asaph and Jeduthun. Heman was the king's seer in respect to the words (? deeds) of God (1 Chron. **25.** 5), and was the leader in matters of worship, whilst the descendants of Moses were at the head of the financial department (1 Chron. **23.** 14–16; **26.** 24).

To sum up this part of our discussion, it may be said, first, that we have not the whole of what Samuel, Nathan, and Gad wrote; secondly, that there were other writers, sacred and secular, in those days; and, thirdly, that our two extant histories of David's times were compiled from first-class historical materials, and were mainly, if not wholly, the compositions of prophetic men.

3. We pass now to the time of SOLOMON. During his reign the sons of Shisha (? Shavsha) were scribes; Jehoshaphat, the son of Ahilud, was still recorder; and Nathan's sons, Azariah and Abud, were in high position (1 Kings **4.** 3–5). Thus continuity was secured; and this would probably be the case to some extent all through the history. *Materials for Solomon's history.*

At the end of Solomon's life we are told (1 Kings **11.** 41) that "the rest of the acts of Solomon, and all that he did, and his wisdom, are they not written in the book of the acts of Solomon?" This is the first appearance of the familiar formula. We have already commented on the word דברים, "acts," which signifies "transactions," whether by word or deed. It is noticeable that the Book of Kings does not profess to give the secular annals. The writer uses what he thinks needful, and refers the purely historical investigator to other sources. It cannot be too clearly affirmed that the Bible, first and last, gives us no annals, properly speaking, but fragments, extracts, selections, put together by inspired men on some special principle.

The chronicler says, " Now the rest of the acts of Solomon, first and last, are they not written in the book of Nathan the prophet, and in the prophecy of Ahijah the Shilonite, and in the visions of Iddo the seer against Jeroboam the son of Nebat" (2 Chron. **9.** 29). Have we, then, here the names of the contributors to the Book of Kings, or of annalists to whom the writer of the Kings refers? Before answering let us inquire, what do we know of these writers? Something has already been said about Nathan. It was he who anointed Solomon king (1 Kings **1.** 10–38), so that he could contribute at any rate the earlier chapters of Solomon's history. Ahijah the prophet, whose head-quarters were at Shiloh, is here said to have written a prophecy. This we still possess in whole or in part in 1 Kings **11.** 31–39, where we have a great promise made to Jeroboam during the lifetime of Solomon. We have another remarkable utterance of his when he was an old man and blind, in the later days of Jeroboam (1 Kings **14.** 6–16). He must have been familiar with the last period of Solomon's life. Iddo's work was of the nature of visions, and he himself is called a visionary. What he had to do with Solomon we cannot tell; but he was a genealogist (see 2 Chron. **12.** 15) and a historian (**13.** 22). There is an old tradition that he was the man of God sent to Bethel, and this would account for the fact that his vision is said to concern Jeroboam the son of Nebat.

If we survey the narrative of Solomon's life in the Book of Kings, we shall see that there is nothing in it which could not have been ascertained by one or other of these three prophets. The history in the Chronicles is almost wholly abstracted from the Kings—perhaps from an enlarged recension of it; but there are slight additions, which probably came from the records of the houses of Asaph, Heman, and Jeduthun. We see no reason to doubt that the authorities cited by the chronicler are those to whom we owe this part of the Kings. They were all prophets, and all had access to Solomon and to his state annals. Their work would dovetail in with that already done for the life of David, one of the authorities for the latter contributing also to the former. We thus see the beginning of a history of the Davidic kingdom, issuing from the hands of a chain of prophetic men whose evidence would be of what we should call first-class value, being contemporary and authoritative.

4. In 1 Kings **14.** 29, we read, "The rest of the acts of *Materials for Reho-* REHOBOAM, and all that he did, are they not written in the *boam's his-* book of the chronicles of the kings of Judah?" Here a *tory.* new expression meets us. The kingdom is divided, and Judah has its special chroniclers. The words translated "chronicles" (דברי הימים) signify "daily acts," or, in one word, "journals." It is the Hebrew name of our Book of Chronicles, but of course this is not the book referred to here. There must have been official annals to which the writer in the Kings refers. In 2 Chron. **12.** 15, we read, "Now the acts of Rehoboam, first and last, are they not written in the book (transactions) of Shemaiah the prophet, and of Iddo the seer concerning genealogies?" What do we know of Shemaiah the prophet? We find him occupying the same sort of position in the days of Rehoboam that Isaiah did in the age of Hezekiah. In 2 Chron. **11.** 2 he is called "the man of God," and he forbids Rehoboam,

in the Lord's name, to go up against Jeroboam; also, in chap. 12. 2 and 7, he expresses the Divine counsel concerning Shishak. Iddo the seer survived Rehoboam, so that he and Shemaiah together were competent to write the history of the reign, and in so doing to continue the work already carried on by Iddo himself in conjunction with Nathan and Ahijah. On examining the materials used by the chronicler we find that he gives a fuller account of some of Rehoboam's proceedings than we possess in our present copies of the Kings; and though the additional matter lies in the compass of twenty verses, it indicates either that the Book of Kings in its original form was a larger work than we have now, or that there were some additional materials still accessible in the chronicler's time.

The history of the later kings.   5. The materials for the history of the succeeding kings may be put together thus :—In the Book of Kings " the chronicles or annals of the kings of Judah " are referred to in connection with the reigns of Abijam, Asa, Jehoram, Amaziah, Azariah, Ahaz, Hezekiah, Manasseh, Amon, Josiah, and Jehoiakim, no reference being made to these annals in the case of Jehoshaphat, Ahaziah, Athaliah, Joash, Jotham, Jehoahaz, Jehoiachin, and Zedekiah. In the Book of Chronicles the story (*midrash*) or history of the prophet Iddo is cited as the authority for Abijam's reign, so that this prophet had to do with at least three successive kings of Judah (see above). The acts of Asa are said to be written " in the book of the kings of Judah and Israel " (2 Chron. 16. 11). What book can this be? Not a volume of official annals, as that would not combine the history of two independent kingdoms, but some such work as we possess in our Book of Kings, only longer than the book is now.

In the case of Jehoshaphat we read that his acts were " written in the book (transactions) of Jehu, the son of Hanani, who is mentioned in the book of the kings of Israel " (2 Chron. 20. 34). Hanani, the seer, is referred to in the times of Asa (2 Chron. **16. 7**), and his remarkable words are preserved to us. Jehu, his son, rebukes Jehoshaphat in the same tone as Hanani had adopted towards Asa, and regardless of the consequence which had ensued in his father's case (2 Chron. **19. 2**). But is he mentioned in the Book of Kings? There is a Jehu, the son of Hanani, mentioned as prophesying against Baasha, Asa's contemporary, in 1 Kings **16. 1, 7, 12**. There cannot be any doubt that he is the same man; so that he and his father were prophets together; and if Jehu was answerable for the reign of Jehoshaphat, he may well have been the authority for the reign of Asa also, though the fact is not mentioned. We take it, therefore, that " the book of the kings of Israel " referred to in 2 Chron. **20. 31** is our Book of Kings in its original form, and that Jehu was one of the chain of prophets who composed it.

The next notice is at the end of the reign of Joash, concerning whom we are told that matters relating to his sons, and the greatness of the burdens on him, and the repairing (Heb. " founding ") of the House of God were to be found written in the story or history (*midrash*) of the Book of the Kings (2 Chron. **24. 27**). There is certainly plenty in our Book of Kings about the burden laid on Joash by Hazael, and concerning his repairing of the Temple, but nothing special about his sons. The LXX. suggests a different reading, in which there would be no reference to his sons.

For Amaziah's reign, as also for the reigns of Jotham, Ahaz, Josiah, and Jehoiakim, we are referred to " the book of the kings of Judah and Israel"; for Uzziah's, to " the historical work of Isaiah "; whilst with regard to the rest of the acts of Hezekiah and his mercies (*i.e.* the mercies shown to him), we are told that they are written in " the vision of Isaiah, the prophet, in the book (עַל־סֵפֶר) of the kings of Judah and Israel." Thus Isaiah is one of the goodly band of historico-prophetic writers to whom we owe the Book of Kings in its original form. Who took up the pen between the prophet Jehu and Isaiah we are not told.

C

Some things in Manasseh's history are said to be written "among (עַל) the sayings of the seers" (2 Chron. 33, 19). The word translated "sayings" is the ordinary one for transactions, and the word rendered "seers" is rightly translated as a proper name in the Revised Version (Hozai), though the interpretation of the Authorized Version is defensible on the supposition of a different reading. Manasseh's reign is given in one single chapter in the Kings, yet it records in outline all that seems referred to in Chronicles, though we evidently have it only in a condensed form.

The kings of Israel.

6. As for the kingdom of Israel, after it split off from that of Judah, it must have had its own annalists, and we judge partly from the analogy of Judah, and partly from what we know concerning the "sons of the prophets" in the days of Elijah and Elisha, that there must have been a chain of prophetic writers, who would record such facts as seemed needful to be preserved from a religious point of view. Their records must have drifted into the possession of the Jewish prophets after the captivity of the Ten Tribes, and were amalgamated with the rest of the work by the final composer of the Book of Kings. This, at least, is a probable theory, but we have no materials for attaining certainty.

Summary.

7. We have thus come to the end of this examination, and we are led to the conclusion that the Books of Samuel and Kings, as we now possess them, are the work of a series of prophets, who were contemporary with the kings whose histories they record; that they were originally longer than they are now, and that they refer to civil annals of the kingdom as having been kept throughout the regal period. With regard to the Chronicles, the writer must have had before him the Book of Kings in its original form, in which there were retained the names of most, if not all, its prophetic composers. There is no sign that the civil annals of the kingdom were preserved when the chronicler did his work, but he apparently had access to certain Levitical documents in addition to the works of the prophetic historians.

CHAPTER V.

INDICATIONS OF A COMPILER'S HAND IN THE LATER HISTORICAL BOOKS.

1. The point we have reached is, that we have contemporary materials from the hands of prophetic or commissioned writers covering the ground between the age of Samuel and that of the Captivity, *i.e.* above four centuries. We must now pursue our investigations in two opposite directions, first completing the period from the Captivity to the age of Nehemiah, and then starting back from the period of Samuel to the books which stand earlier in our Bibles.

We do not know when the Books of Samuel and Kings *Completion of the Book of Kings.* attained their present form, but we have no reason to doubt that the last chief contributor to them was the prophet JEREMIAH; and he may have been the compiler of the whole. If the student will read attentively 2 Kings **24.** 18 to **25.** 30, and will compare it verse by verse with Jer. **52.** 1–34, he will not have any doubt that he has two copies of the same document before him.* There is, indeed, one section of seven verses omitted in the latter document, and there are several minute variations; but otherwise both the substance and the words are the same. The case is somewhat similar to that of Isaiah, who was an earlier contributor to the Book of Kings. We find incorporated in his Book of Visions certain parts of his biographical or historical works, especially those which bear on the great scheme of his prophecy. And just as the story of the Divine intervention on behalf of Hezekiah furnishes an admirable historical foreground for Isaiah's prophecies

---

* It is not, however, certain that the last chapter of Jeremiah is from the prophet's pen. See chap. 51 *fin.*

of the great salvation, so Jeremiah's own narrative of the Captivity seems a fitting close to the pathetic appeals which make up the great part of his prophecies.

Possibly Jeremiah's work.

2. On the whole, we feel justified in supposing—though it is only an hypothesis—that Jeremiah took with him to Egypt the series of historical documents which he had inherited from the sons of the prophets, and that he compiled the whole work in Egypt with the aid of Baruch and other scribes. Still certain questions rise in our mind. How, for example, did the compiler get the last sentences which concern the thirty-seventh year of the captivity of Jehoiachin? This must have been added by a later hand. Again, how did his compilation get into the hands of the author of the Chronicles, or of the composer of Ezra, or of the prophet Daniel? The answer is a very simple one. There was free intercourse between Egypt and the East all through this period. The Jews in Babylon and those in Egypt would have frequent communications with each other; and not only letters but books could safely be conveyed from country to country.

Compila-tion of the Chronicles.

3. We now pass on to the Book of Chronicles, which must have been compiled during or after the Captivity. In the last portion of the book we find extracts freely made from the Kings, as in the earlier parts; also, Jeremiah is referred to, both as lamenting over Josiah, as warning Zedekiah, and as prophesying concerning the Seventy years; so that the chronicler knew both the historical and the prophetical works of Jeremiah.

Relation of Chronicles to Ezra.

There is a curious phenomenon at the close of the Second Book of Chronicles. It would seem naturally to have ended at the twenty-first verse of the thirty-sixth chapter, where we are told that the land enjoyed her Sabbaths for seventy years. The writer, however, or some later editor, appends the first sentences of the Book of Ezra, actually breaking off in the middle of a verse. Perhaps this appendage was not part of the original document. It presupposes not only that Cyrus' edict had been issued, but that the particular account of it with which Ezra begins his book was in existence.

Some critics jump to the conclusion that whoever wrote Ezra must have written the Chronicles. But this by no means follows. Many books may have had a few words added by a later hand in order to give completeness to them, or even so as to suggest what book should be read next in historical order. It might even be that some copyist in very early times, having Chronicles and Ezra before him written as one work, overran the true end of the Chronicles. The passage, however, looks like a deliberate insertion, intended to show the fulfilment of God's word uttered by Isaiah and Jeremiah; and in that case it needs no further comment.

As to the actual authorship of the Chronicles, it will be best to leave it open, but certainly there are strong reasons for attributing it to Ezra. We should expect by the analogy of the earlier Historical Books, and from some peculiarities in the contents, that it is the work of one who combined in himself the position of a prophet, the lineage of a Levite or priest, and perhaps the office of a genealogist. All these things point to such an one as Ezra, but they are not absolutely conclusive. There are reasons why it is improbable that Daniel, Haggai, or Zechariah wrote the book. Some of these would equally militate against the hypothesis *The Two Parts of Ezra.* that the compiler of the First Part of the Book of Ezra was the author. This First Part is in the main a series of official documents threaded together with a slight personal narrative, and was probably put together by order of Jeshua (*i.e.* Joshua), the High Priest. Ezra himself is personally answerable only for the Second Part of the book which bears his name (*i.e.* chaps. 7–10). He included in it various lists of names which were written out for him by subordinates, *e.g.* the lists of those who had taken strange wives (chap. 10. 18–24). He also prefixed what we may call the Jeshua-narrative, and made the two into one book.

Nehemiah. 4. The Book of Nehemiah is to that of Ezra very much what the work of Nathan may have been to that of Gad in composing the history of David. Nehemiah was a vigorous, practical man, and, we imagine, not much of a writer, but he kept a narrative of God's dealings with him and through him, and of his own heart's aspirations towards God; and this narrative we possess. The book contains some documents, *e.g.* the list of repairers of the Temple, and—most important of all—an extract (chap. **7**. 6–73) from the Jeshua-narrative contained in the Book of Ezra. At first sight we should be inclined to think that Jeshua and Nehemiah had two independent copies made from one Temple document. We cannot account, on any theory, for the numerous textual variations which we observe on comparing the two. These we must look at when discussing the state of the text. But it is clear that Nehemiah's scribe or clerk used what we call the Jeshua-narrative rather than the materials from which it was composed as his authority; for in copying he overran the list which he was ordered to copy, possibly owing to the similarity of certain words. The second chapter of Ezra ends thus:—"and the Nethinims dwelt in their cities, and all Israel in their cities." The third chapter begins thus:—" And when the seventh month was come, and the children of Israel were in their cities." Nehemiah's copyist would naturally have ended where Ezra's second chapter ends; but the student will see, if he turns to Neh. **7**. 73, that the copyist ran on into the first sentence of the next section.

Other materials may be detected in Nehemiah. Thus the remarkable address to God in the ninth chapter is one of a large class of addresses and prayers which must have been committed to paper by qualified hearers. The lists of names in the later chapters are also copied from official documents, some (see, *e.g.*, the reference to Jaddua, chap. **12**. 11, 22) being probably added at a later time.

We need not go further into details. Many points are left unsettled, but we see that the Books of Ezra and Nehemiah are partly extracts from contemporary works and partly autobiographical. They are thus first-class authorities for the history of the period, and form a fitting appendix to the earlier Historical Books.

We have omitted all questions relating to the genealogies, which must be returned to in a later part of our discussion.

5. We have now attained a sure critical and historical *Summary.* standing-ground, consisting of a series of historical documents reaching back from the days of Nehemiah to the inception of the kingdom of Israel under Samuel. Although they present but a sketch of the history, and that mainly for a religious purpose, yet they are unequalled for the insight they give us into the inner and outer life of an ancient people during a period of six centuries. We must not pause at present to consider their contents, but must stand on their furthest edge and gaze back into the pre-existing state of things. Here we are primarily confronted with the Books of Joshua and Judges, and our business must be to inquire whether they show signs of compilation like those which we have been already considering.

CHAPTER VI.

MARKS OF COMPILATION IN THE EARLIEST BOOKS.

Materials for the Book of Joshua. 1. The Book of JOSHUA is largely autobiographical, though written in the third person. The first part of it covers but a few years, and is vivid, and abounding with topographical details of proved accuracy. The later chapters, containing the boundary-lists, &c., are largely compiled from documents which we may have to discuss later on. The speeches towards the end must have been preserved in substance, if not verbally, by the *sopherim*, or scribes, who were specially appointed and qualified for this class of work. Who finally compiled the book we know not. The greater part may have been put together by order of Joshua and preserved in the Tabernacle archives, and Phinehas, the son of Eleazar, the son of Aaron, may have completed the history. This is in the main the old view of the book.

Materials for the Book of Judges. The case of the JUDGES is very different from that of Joshua. It covers a period of some four centuries, so that no one person could be answerable for the whole. Here we see the advantage of having the analogy of the later Historical Books to help us. In the light which they afford, it seems most probable that the leading sketches preserved in the Book of Judges were recorded by a series of officials, priestly or otherwise, the book itself being compiled at the close of the period, possibly by Samuel. It is fairly open to discussion whether this theory fits the facts as a whole, or whether it must give way to something newer and better. Whoever compiled the book must have had access not only to the Shiloh archives, but to family memorials, and to the collection of songs and folk-lore which may have gone under the title of "the Book of Jasher" (see Josh. **10.** 13 and 2 Sam. **1.** 18). This last-named book may have included such sections as the Song of Deborah and Barak, and the fable or parable of Jotham. The Book of Judges is not in complete chronological order. The last five chapters refer to events of a comparatively early date, when Phinehas the son of Eleazar, the son of Aaron, was still ministering before the Ark.

2. The relationship of the Book of Judges to that of Joshua is specially to be noted. There is a modern theory that Joshua is much the later of the two. Whether this be so or not we need not now discuss, for it is evidently an abstruse question. But there is this remarkable phenomenon, that the first two chapters of the Judges make free use of certain materials which are to be found *verbatim*, though not always in the same order, in Joshua. (See Judg. **1.** 10–15, 20, 21, 27, 28, and **2.** 6–9; and compare the references to chaps. **15, 16, 19, 23,** and **24** of Joshua throughout.) We thus get a case of the overlapping of books somewhat similar to others that we have already observed. It is not only that the facts recorded are the same, but that the language is the same. We have indubitable *quotations* in Judges, either from Joshua or from the materials in the hands of the compiler of Joshua. These passages are all of the same class; they point to the existence of archives at Shechem, Mizpeh, or Shiloh, at which a record of the leading facts in the history of Israel were preserved. *Relation-ship between Judges and Joshua.*

3. Once more we shall have to step back, and this time it is from the Books of Joshua and Judges to the ancient documents which preceded them, our object being, as before, simply to look for indications of materials out of which the history might be composed. It must be borne in mind that we are at present dealing with the substance of the books, not with the *minutiæ*. We are not discussing the use of particular Hebrew words, or the names of God, or questions of style. These must be dealt with later on. We began with the unquestionable fact that the central body of the Historical Books claims to be of the nature of a compilation from contemporary prophetic sources; we then saw that the *Recapitula-tion.*

Books of Ezra and Nehemiah bore the marks of compilation; that the Book of Judges, if historical, as we hold it to be, must from the nature of the case be a compilation, covering as it does a period of several centuries; and that Joshua contains indications of having been composed partly from autobiographical records, and partly from official documents.

We ought to add that there is no way whereby the Hebrew writers mark quotations or extracts. No brackets, no inverted commas, are used in the Sacred Books; and it is comparatively seldom, except in cases which we have already fully discussed, that the writers mention their authorities. It is quite clear, however, as anyone can see for himself if he will make a full collation of the Chronicles with Samuel and Kings, that the chronicler felt himself at liberty to make free use of the older documents which lay before him. Nor did he hesitate to alter, whether in the way of modification, compression, or expansion, the older documents which lay before him, or to blend into one account the materials which he obtained from two or more sources. Thus the value of the Book of Chronicles to the modern critic is immense. Without it we should be at a loss concerning many points of literary and historic interest. It establishes an important precedent, and throws light backward on the earlier books, and forward as far as the Gospels.

The Pentateuch. 4. It is our business now, in the light of the results already attained, to go back to the PENTATEUCH. We are not ashamed of the name. We treat it—as venerable tradition invites us to treat it—as one work, which has travelled down through the ages from the period in which Israel entered Canaan. If it is not so to be treated; if the traditional view is to be wholly set aside; if large portions of the Pentateuch are to be brought down centuries later than the age of Moses, as some critics affirm—well, we are prepared to examine the evidence. The burden of proof will manifestly lie with the critic who seeks to disintegrate; it must be strong; it must be overwhelming.

The last four books of which the Pentateuch is composed are manifestly of a different character from the first. They give us the transactions of one man and the history of one age; whilst Genesis gives us an outline of the history of the world in general, and of the Abrahamic family in particular, up to the time when Exodus begins. Each book, however, may be considered separately, and, according to our usual method, we will begin with the last.

5. The Book of DEUTERONOMY is mainly compiled from *Materials for Deuteronomy.* the speeches or sermons delivered by Moses at the end of his life to the generation of Israelites who had risen up during the Wanderings in the Desert. The time and the place in which these addresses were given are exactly specified in the first verses of the book. They would be taken down by the qualified scribes of the period, and by the order of Moses, who felt that whilst he was speaking God was speaking through him. Their contents are partly historical, partly legislative, and, being delivered orally, they were specially adapted to the hearts and circumstances of the people whom he addressed. At the close of the book we have the song which all Israel was to learn by heart, and which is more frequently referred to in later books of the Bible than any other section of the Pentateuch. We also have the blessing of the Tribes and the death of Moses. The compilation of the book must have been an easy task. With Deut. 32. 44 before us, we naturally look to Joshua as taking authority from Moses for producing such a book, though its actual compilation would have been the work of scribes.

6. The Book of NUMBERS has a prefatory notice of time *Materials for Numbers.* and place in the first verse, and a postscript at the close. Its narrative starts from the beginning of the second year of the Wanderings, when the people were in Sinai, and it leaves off at the close of the forty years, in the plain of Moab, just where Deuteronomy begins. Thirty-eight years are passed over without a word between the 19th and 20th chapters.

The book is mainly compiled from lists, standing orders, and other documents, interspersed with fragments of history and song, and with records of legislative acts which professedly were revealed by God to Moses. The references to "The Book of the Wars of the Lord" and to "The Proverbs" in the 21st chapter, remind us that there was growing up amongst the people a literature of their own, alongside of the Sacred Books, probably poetical in its structure, partly of the same class as the works of the celebrated Egyptian poet Pentaur, and partly to be compared with the adventures of the Mohar, with whom Egyptologists have made us familiar. This fact helps us to understand better what a wealth of materials may have been in the hands of the compiler of the Book of Judges in later times. Even as far down in time as the age of Jeremiah, these songs may still have been current among the people, though he *may* have got his extracts solely from the Book of Numbers (comp. Num. 21. 28, 29, with Jer. 48. 45, 46). Some think that the insertions in the Book of Numbers are borrowed from Jeremiah! Such an assertion might be swallowed, but hardly digested. Let the student put the documents side by side and read them attentively, and draw his own conclusions.

The real puzzle in the Book of Numbers is the narrative concerning Balaam. How were his utterances obtained by the compiler of Numbers? There are linguistic peculiarities in these chapters which may be touched upon in a later stage of our inquiry, and for the present we must rest content with two suppositions drawn from analogy: first, that Balaam's utterances were recorded by himself or his scribes; secondly, that they were obtained by Moses before or during the overthrow of the Midianites, when Balaam was slain (Num. 31. 8).

Materials for Leviticus.

7. The Book of LEVITICUS is professedly made up of the series of decrees and statutes revealed to Moses. The first half of the book has *formulæ* concerning the authorship of the materials, with postscripts at the close of each class of

ordinance. These will readily be detected by the student. Thus, let him trace the formula " The Lord spake to Moses, saying." There are also two summaries at the close of the book (chaps. **26.** 46 and **27.** 34), which show that the period covered by the book closes just where the Book of Numbers begins.

All the rubrical directions and ordinances contained in Leviticus must have been written by scribes at the command of Moses. The few historical episodes in the book would be the work of the recorders. The greater part, if not the whole, of the materials would thus be prepared under the authorization of Moses, who may fairly be credited with the book itself.

8. The Book of EXODUS ends where Leviticus begins. *Materials for Exodus.* The first parts consists of family and autobiographical records, including the whole story of the Exodus. There is a certain amount of legislation which finds its natural place in the narrative. There is also the specification of the Tabernacle and its furniture, together with the report of its construction in almost identical language, whilst the episode of the Golden Calf lies embedded amidst these documents. On reviewing the book we see no substantial part which could not have been either written or authorized by Moses, from materials of the same class as those which we find in later books.

9. Only the Book of GENESIS remains, and that stands at *The Book of Genesis.* the head of the Old Testament, as the most venerable of Biblical documents. How can we deal with this ancient book ? Who can have composed it ? and from what materials ? We have already, earlier in this chapter, called attention to the fact that we must not look for external marks of a compiler's hand, whether mechanical or literary. It would indeed have made our researches a very easy matter if we had been told at the end of Genesis that the volume was written by such and such a person and at such a time ; or if we had been told at the beginning of Exodus that Moses wrote or compiled Genesis from previous sources ;

but we have no such help. We must therefore examine the contents of the books, and judge them by the analogy of those which we have already discussed.

Its main character-istic.

Genesis contains fifty chapters. All but the first eleven of these form a fairly consecutive though fragmentary history of Abraham, his son, his grandson, and that grandson's family. They abound in vivid personal detail. They are old-world stories now; and they were old-world stories in the days of the Exodus. They are threaded to one another as some of the later narratives are, *e.g.* Nehemiah's book. They are all religious in their tone and character, and are professedly a story not so much of a family as of God's dealings with the family. And this, it may be noticed in passing, is the case with all the later Historical Books. They all tell of what purport to be Divine promises, expressions of a Divine purpose, towards the individual, the family, the nation, the world. This is essentially *the* characteristic of the whole, and it at once suggests the secret of the compilation.

Divine revelation and inter-vention.

Let us suppose, what is at least a possible hypothesis, that God did indeed form a plan (to use human words concerning infinite mysteries) whereby the greatest needs of the human race should be satisfied, and that with a view to the carrying out of that plan it should be deemed wise to choose a particular land wherein certain great deeds should be done, and a particular nation amongst whom primarily the Divine method of intervention should be realized. Let us suppose, what is equally possible, that this same Divine Being should prepare the way for the great event, through a long period, by means of a series of lesser interventions, self-manifestations, and utterances, all more or less related to each other, as proceeding from a common source, and all tending to produce distinct impressions on the mind concerning God's nature, moral government, and willingness to enter into close and helpful relations with His children. Lastly, let us suppose, what will be most natural under the circumstances, and what we have already shown to be possible from a literary point of view, viz., that the heads of the family with whom God thus came into special relation should preserve accounts of His dealings with them, stage by stage. Then, if those documents could be preserved, we should have the materials from which the Book of Genesis (from the twelfth chapter and onwards) might be compiled.

This, then, is our hypothesis. Is it not a good working hypothesis? Is it not a fair and reasonable one? Has any one any *primâ facie* objection to it? If so, on what grounds is that objection raised? *A rational hypothesis.*

10. There remain the first eleven chapters of Genesis to be dealt with. They contain the narratives of the Creation, the Fall, the Deluge, and the Dispersion. We are now in pre-Patriarchal times, when the art of writing was in its infancy; we have ascended the stream of history to its mysterious source. Yet here we have the same style of document as in the later books, *e.g.* vivid details, some honourable, some shameful, concerning Noah and his family; and genealogies, taking us back like stepping-stones through the centuries, till we find ourselves standing outside the misty gates of Paradise in company with the first parents of our race. These primæval people speak—we know not in what tongue—they hold communion with their Creator; they have Law, Punishment, Covenant, Light, Hope. All of these come to them through the self-manifestation of Him in Whom they lived and moved and had their being. From Him *may* have come direct to them the story—told as one might tell it to a child—of the origin of all things; a bare outline but strictly theistic. From Him they may have drawn not only the gift of speech but the instinct which led them to pass on to others the story of their creation and of their shame, together with the sure Promise of Redemption. *The pre-Patriarchal age.*

11. When writing became possible, which may have been in antediluvian times, the story, which was oral, would be sketched in few and simple words on tablets or on bricks, *Transmission of primæval truth.*

From Noah to Abraham. in Accadian or some other primæval tongue. In course of time Abraham was selected to be the head of the family in which all the nations of the earth should be blessed; and there would be no difficulty in his becoming possessor of trustworthy copies or translations of these documents, which would thenceforward be handed down to his posterity, and from these, or such as these, the early part of Genesis would be composed, the whole series being welded into one by some qualified person, into whose keeping the documents would come on the death of Joseph. Who would this person be? Can there be any doubt?

From Joseph to Moses. When Israel came out of Egypt they carried the embalmed body of Joseph with them, and with that precious historical relic would naturally be deposited the archives of his house. Thus the whole materials for Genesis would come into the hands of MOSES, and from his hands it is reasonable to believe they passed—probably more or less in their present form—into the safe keeping of Joshua.

This is all hypothesis. But, we ask again, is it not reasonable? It presupposes, indeed, one thing all the way through, viz., the existence of a living God, with feelings, and mind, and power, and wisdom, capable of planning and of carrying out His plans, capable of intervening in behalf of His children, capable also of communicating such parts of His purposes as He thought fit to certain selected persons. If this is granted, the literary difficulties that lie before us will be easily overcome. On any non-theistic hypothesis the critic and the historian will be alike nonplussed.

Summary. 12. We take it, then, as possible—nay, as probable—that whilst the Books of Exodus, Leviticus, Numbers, and Deuteronomy were compiled either by Moses or from official materials which Moses authorized, the Book of Genesis is based upon contemporary materials, which had accumulated in the hands of the Patriarchs from the beginning, and which were threaded together, under Divine enlightenment, by the most capable man of ancient times.

CHAPTER VII.

WHAT WAS NEHEMIAII'S BIBLE?

1. We have now secured a standing-ground which justifies *Tests of age and integrity needed.* us in proceeding to further and more exact investigations. We have found a body of literature which may not unreasonably be regarded as based in the main on the records of con- temporaries, extending back from the days of Nehemiah to those of Samuel, and, with less certain evidence, from the time of Samuel to that of the Exodus, whilst further back still stands the Book of Genesis. How can we further test the age and integrity of such ancient books?

2. It may be well to ask what course is taken with regard *Analogy of the New Testament.* to the somewhat analogous case of the New Testament. If we wish to examine the age and integrity of any book in this "Christian Library," what course do we adopt? We first investigate the age of the manuscripts, then we study the antiquity and contents of the oldest versions, and finally we examine with the greatest care the quotations in early Christian writings. It is these on which we are specially dependent. Anyone can see this for himself by studying Dr. Westcott's work on *The Canon,* or Dr. Sanday's *Gospels in the Second Century.*

The same course may fairly be adopted with regard to *Difficulty in case of the Old Testament.* the Old Testament, so far as it is practicable. But here we find ourselves in a far more difficult position. We have absolutely no pre-Christian MSS. of these ancient books. The only pre-Christian versions are the Septuagint and the Samaritan Pentateuch, to which may be appended, though doubtfully, the earliest of the Chaldee Targums or Para- phrases on the Pentateuch and some other books. But with the possible exception of the Samaritan documents, whose age and authority are not well established, and which it is customary now to ignore, none of these go back beyond

D

the age of Nehemiah, which is our starting-point. We are thus thrown chiefly, if not wholly, on the third method of testing ancient books, viz., the use made of them by the succeeding writers. Accordingly, starting from the period of Nehemiah, we have to inquire how far a more ancient literature is presupposed in his time; then we go further back and renew the question again and again until we find ourselves landed in the earliest of all the books.

Quotations.   3. The study of quotations is quite a science. We have to be on our guard against mistaking resemblances for references. Some expressions may be common property to several Hebrew writers; they may have almost become idioms in the language; and we cannot say that the writers borrowed them from one another. Also, there are proverbial expressions common to two writers which cannot fairly be called quotations. Again, it is not always possible to demonstrate in some cases which of two writers quotes from the other. Lastly, the English version often misleads; it translates different Hebrew words in the same way, and the same Hebrew word in different ways, so that every supposed or possible quotation has to be determined in the light of the original. Even when all these safeguards have been attended to it remains to be inquired how far quotations from a book are tests of its integrity (*i.e.* entirety) at the time in which the quotation is made. It is generally acknowledged, however, that in the case of books of authority and of a religious character two or three quotations go a long way to establish the position of the book as a whole.

And now we must embark on this difficult but interesting task. We take the Books of EZRA and NEHEMIAH in our hands, and ask ourselves if they presuppose or refer to any earlier literature; if so, of what class is it? and to what extent is it referred to?

Quotations and references in Ezra 1–6.   4. The first part of the Book of Ezra, which we have called the Jeshua-narrative, opens with a reference to the

prophecy of Jeremiah. It deals with a state of things, and
with tribes, families, and genealogies, which all presuppose
some such accounts as are given in Samuel, Kings, and
Chronicles. Thus, we have not only references to the
Captivity which took place in the age of Nebuchadnezzar,
but also to the system of worship established in the time
of David, whose ordinances and whose formulæ of praise
are specifically referred to (see Ezra **3.** 10, 11), whilst the
references to the family of Barzillai the Gileadite and to the
descendants of Asaph take us back genealogically to the same
period. The writings of Moses, the man of God, are also
referred to (Ezra **3.** 2 and **6.** 18) as the authority for the re-
establishment of the altar, the morning and evening burnt
offerings, the feast of tabernacles, and various other set feasts.

When we look at the brevity of the narrative, which is
almost made up of official documents, this is as much as
we could reasonably expect; but we also find a reference in
Ezra **5.** 1 and **6.** 14 to the prophets Haggai and Zechariah,
whose writings may therefore be included in the evidence of
this period. In Haggai **1.** 6 we read, " Ye have sown much
and bring in little ; ye eat, but ye have not enough." Here
we have manifest quotations from Deut. **28.** 38 and Lev.
26. 26, whilst in Zech. **2.** 8 we have strong reason to
recognize a quotation from the Memorial Song (Deut. **32.**
10), " He kept him as the apple of his eye." Zechariah
also refers to the ancient and oft-repeated promise which
originates in Exod. **6.** 7, where we read, " I will take you
to Me for a people, and I will be to you for a God "
(Zech. **8.** 8). Passing over minor references (*e.g.* Zech.
8. 12), and those about which there might be fair difference
of opinion, it is important to notice the three references to
the words of "the former prophets" as having been uttered
under the influence of God's Spirit, and having been fulfilled
in the punishment of the people (Zech. **1.** 4; **7.** 7, 12).

Putting all this together, we see that when Israel returned
from captivity (*circ.* B.C. 536–521) the leaders of the people
not only had amongst them prophets of God, but were

D 2

apparently familiar with at least some of the writings which are contained in the Pentateuch and which claimed Moses as the author, as well as with the ordinances which date back only as far as David.

Quotations and references in Ezra 7-10.

5. The next period (70 years later) is that of Ezra and Nehemiah. Here we find ourselves in company with a ready scribe in the Law of Moses, who was familiar with the words of the Commandments of the Lord and His statutes. He had a most difficult task to perform; for "the holy seed" had mingled itself with the people of the land. In his prayer over the matter (Ezra 9) he refers to the injunctions given by "God's servants the prophets," and summarizes them in words which may be illustrated from such passages as Exod. 34. 16 and Deut. 7. 3. He uses one remarkable expression in the course of this prayer, when he says that the Canaanites had filled the land "from one end to another" with their uncleanness. Literally, the words are "from mouth to mouth." It may have been a common idiom, but it is only to be found elsewhere in 2 Kings 21. 16, where "God's servants the prophets" are referred to (verse 10), and Manasseh is reported as having filled Jerusalem (with blood) "from one end to another." There is nothing improbable in the idea that Ezra, being a ready scribe, had this passage in his mind whilst praying.

Quotations and references in Nehemiah.

6. Nehemiah's prayer (Neh. 1) is remarkable not only for its adaptation of words which though springing from Exodus are to be found *verbatim* in Daniel (compare Neh. 1. 5 with Dan. 9. 4), but also for its deliberate quotation from "the word commanded by God to His servant Moses," and it illustrates a tendency which we find in the New Testament writers, as also in Justin Martyr and others, which led them to combine two or three passages into one. The extract from Moses given in Nehemiah runs thus:—"If ye transgress, I will scatter you among the nations: But if ye return unto Me, and keep My commandments, and do them; though there were of you cast out unto the uttermost part of the

heaven, yet I will gather them from thence, and will bring
them unto the place that I have chosen to set My name
there. Now these are thy servants and thy people, whom
thou hast redeemed by thy great power, and by thy strong
hand." This is how the words stand in what we take to be
Nehemiah's own record. There is no doubt that Nehemiah
confidently referred to the words, first, as having come down
from Moses, and, secondly, as having been put into Moses'
mouth by God. Whence are they taken? In Deut. **30.** 1–4
we read:—" When all these things are come upon thee . . .
and thou shalt call them to mind among all the nations
whither the Lord thy God hath driven thee, and shalt return
unto the Lord thy God, and shalt obey His voice according
to all that I command thee this day, then . . . the Lord will
turn thy captivity . . . and will return and gather thee from
all the nations whither the Lord thy God hath scattered thee.
If any of thine be driven out unto the outmost parts of heaven, from thence will the Lord thy God gather thee." The
earlier words, " I will scatter thee among the nations " are
from Lev. **26.** 33, and the expression " the place which I
have chosen to put My name there " may be illustrated from
Deut. **12.** 21; **16.** 11, and other passages.

In Nehemiah **8,** Ezra is called upon to bring the Book of
the Law of Moses which the Lord commanded to Israel. In
accordance with what the people read in it, they kept the
feast of tabernacles, as had been done ninety years before
(Ezra **3.** 4). The particular passage which they must have
read is Lev. **23.** 39–43, on the strength of which they published in the cities that the people should fetch olive, pine,
myrtle, and palm branches, with the branches of thick trees,
and they had such a dwelling in booths as had not been
observed " since the days of Jeshua (*i.e.* Joshua) the son of
Nun " (Neh. **8.** 17).

We now reach Nehemiah **9,** in which we find a prayer or *Neh.* 9.
address to God worthy of our most careful study. God is
approached as the Maker and Preserver of heaven and earth,
with all that is therein. It is He that chose Abram, called

him Abraham, found him faithful, made a covenant with him, promised the land of Canaan to his seed, saw the affliction of the people in Egypt, heard their cry by the Red Sea, showed signs and wonders on Pharaoh and his servants, divided the sea so that the people went through on dry land, while the enemy sank as a stone; led Israel in the day by a cloudy pillar, and in the night by a pillar of fire; came down on Mount Sinai and gave judgments and statutes and the holy Sabbath, by the hand of Moses; gave bread from heaven, and water out of the rock, for forty years, during which time the people's clothes waxed not old and their feet swelled not; exercised His attributes of grace, mercy, and slowness to anger, even though they made a molten calf and said, This is thy god that brought thee up out of Egypt. Finally, He brought them into Canaan, giving them houses, wells, vineyards, and olive grounds, so they did eat, and were filled, and became fat. So far we have a sketch of the Pentateuch, with a number of verbal quotations from Genesis, Exodus, and Deuteronomy. The prayer goes on to refer to the numerous troubles which befell the people through their sins, to the warnings given by God's Spirit in the Prophets, and to the saviours raised up by God from time to time to deliver the people from their enemies.

The more attentively we analyse the words of the prayer contained in this chapter, the more clearly we see the answer to the important question, What was Nehemiah's Bible? He must have had very much the same Scriptures as the Jews had in our Lord's time, and as we have in the Old Testament.

Further quotations and references. Later in the book we have references to God's Law given by Moses the servant of God, and to various rites, offices, and duties, such as the Sabbath, the Sabbatical year, the shewbread, the meat offering, the burnt offering, the sin offering, the dedication of the firstfruits, the firstborn, and tithes. We also find mention of the descendants of Asaph and Jeduthun, with whose names we are familiar in the Book of Chronicles; and the particular duties of the singers are mentioned as being to praise and give thanks " according to the commandment of David the man of God," where we seem to have a reference to 1 Chron. **23, 25,** and **26.**

There is a "Book of Chronicles" named in Neh. **12. 23.** The words run thus :—" The sons of Levi, even the chief of the fathers, (were) written in the book of the Chronicles, also on to the days of Johanan the son of Eliashib." The reference may have been to our Book of Chronicles (see 1 Chron. **9.** 14–34) ; if so, the passage indicates that the genealogies were continued after the completion of the Book of Chronicles by some authorized person up to the time of Eliashib.

There is one other important passage to be noticed, viz., the beginning of the 13th chapter, where we find that, in the course of reading " the Book of Moses," the people came to the 23rd chapter of Deuteronomy, and found that " the Ammonite and Moabite should not come into the congregation of God for ever, because they met not the children of Israel with bread and with water, but turned Balaam against them that he should curse them, howbeit our God turned the curse into a blessing." The passage is a full and clear instance of a quotation. The effect produced by the reading of it was remarkable. It caused a great separation to be made between Israel and all the mixed multitude, the passage being manifestly regarded as the expression of the mind of God.

7. There are other references, *e.g.* to king Solomon, who *Summary.* was "beloved of God," but entangled by "outlandish women " (Neh. **13.** 26) ; but the student has sufficient materials before him to lead to the conclusion that Nehemiah firmly believed—in company with Ezra and the writer of the Joshua-narrative—that the various branches of legislation contained in the Pentateuch came from God by the hand of Moses. A record of the leading outlines of the history of the people from Abraham onwards was in their hands. In a word, either the Historical Books which we possess, or documents very like them, were in existence at the period of the Return and the Restoration, and were regarded as trustworthy and authoritative.

CHAPTER VIII.

Quotations and references in the Chronicles.

1. The materials from which the Books of CHRONICLES are compiled presuppose, not only Samuel and the Kings, but almost all the earlier books of the Bible. The first chapter might have been composed from Genesis. The genealogical lists which follow bristle with references to the preceding books. Thus we read of " Achar the troubler of Israel " (1 Chron. 2. 7), Jehoshuah the son of Non (7. 27), Bezaleel the son of Uri (2. 20), Gershom and Eliezer the sons of Moses (23. 15), Othniel the son of Kenaz (4. 13), Caleb the son of Jephunneh (4. 15), Shelah the son of Judah (4. 21), Ehud (7. 10), Reuben the firstborn, who defiled his father's bed, and whose birthright was given to the sons of Joseph, while Judah prevailed above his brethren (5. 1, 2 ; compare 28. 4, which shows how David interpreted and applied Jacob's blessing of Judah). So we read of the service of the Aaronic priesthood, the leading outlines of which are specified in 1 Chron. 6. 49 as being carried out " in accordance with all that Moses, the servant of God, commanded " (compare chap. 23. 28–32). The dwelling-places of the priests (1 Chron. 6. 54–81) are taken from a copy of Josh. 21, or from the materials on which that chapter was based. Again, we find a reference to the old promise that God would multiply Israel like the stars of heaven (27. 23) ; and David encourages Solomon in words taken from the first chapter of Joshua : " Be strong and of good courage . . . fear not nor be dismayed, for the Lord God is with thee ; He will not fail thee nor forsake thee " (compare 1 Chron. 28. 20 with Josh. 1. 5 and 9).

The Tabernacle of the Congregation is described as made

by Moses, the servant of the Lord, in the wilderness
(2 Chron. **1.** 3); the brazen altar as having being constructed by Bezaleel the son of Uri (**1.** 5); the Temple is
planned on lines which presuppose the Tabernacle; some of
the Tabernacle furniture is used, notably the Ark containing
"the two tables which Moses put therein at Horeb, when
the Lord made a covenant with the children of Israel, when
they came out of Egypt" (**5.** 10). Solomon's offerings are
presented in accordance with the ritual prescribed by Moses
(**8.** 13, &c.). The Book of the Law of the Lord, *i.e.* copies
of it, were taken about the country by the Levites under
Jehoshaphat's direction; and one Levite at least in those
days was well read in the story of the Exodus, for he
exhorts Judah at a critical period of their history, in words
borrowed from the Exodus, "Stand still and see the salvation
of the Lord" (compare 2 Chron. **20.** 17 with Exod. **14.** 13).

The "collection" which Moses, the servant of God, laid
upon Israel in the wilderness is referred to in 2 Chron. **24.**
6, 9; and when Amaziah refrained from killing the children
of his father's murderers we are told that this was "in
accordance with what is written in the law in the book of
Moses, where the Lord commanded, saying, The fathers shall
not die for the children, neither shall the children die for the
fathers, but every man shall die for his own sin" (compare
2 Chron. **25.** 4 with Deut. **24.** 6).

The Passover is ordered to be kept "as it was written,"
as also the feast of unleavened bread, in Hezekiah's times
(2 Chron. **30.** 5, 13, 16, 18), and in the touching address sent
by the king to all the tribes (**30.** 6-9), God is not only described as the God of Abraham, Isaac, and Israel, *i.e.* as the
God of the Patriarchs, but also as "gracious and merciful"
—words taken from Exod. **34.** 6.

The punishment due to the utter negligence of the people
in the days of king Manasseh, when "the law, the statutes,
and the ordinances by the hand of Moses" were wholly dis-
regarded (**33.** 8), is temporarily warded off in the time of
Josiah, half a century later, when the Law is discovered as a

new thing; the writings of Moses, David, and Solomon are revived and acted upon (see chap. **35**. 4, 6, 12); and the Passover was once more kept as it had not been since the days of Samuel the prophet.

It may be said, however, that Chronicles is a late book, and that all these references only illustrate the chronicler's way of putting things. To this we answer, first, that many of the passages are not ways of putting things, but are professedly history; and, secondly, that many of them will be found to be in the old pre-existing materials which we still possess in the Book of Kings, and which we have seen reason to accept as mainly the works of contemporary writers.

Quotations and references in the Kings. 2. Let us look at a few further illustrations of our present subject from the KINGS. David's parting words to Solomon, given in 1 Kings **2**. 2–4, are not the same as those we have cited from the Chronicles, but they show his familiarity with Deuteronomy and Joshua (compare 1 Kings **2**. 2 with Josh. **23**. 14, and verse 3 with Deut. **29**. 9). The Book of Joshua is specially referred to in 1 Kings **16**. 34, where we read, " In his (Ahab's) days did Hiel the Bethelite build Jericho: he laid the foundation thereof in Abiram his firstborn, and set up the gates thereof in his youngest son Segub, according to the word of the Lord, which He spake by Joshua the son of Nun " (see Josh. **6**. 26).

In the striking account of Elijah's offering (1 Kings **18**) which " ascended " at the time of the evening " Minchah," Elijah took twelve stones, according to the number of the tribes of Jacob, unto whom the word of the Lord came, saying, " Israel shall be thy name " (see Gen. **32**. 28). Afterwards he pleads to have his life taken away, in words he may have read in the Pentateuch (compare 1 Kings **19**. 4 with Num. **11**. 15); he comes to " Horeb, the Mount of God " (see Exod. **3**. 1); and he is there "forty days and forty nights," as Moses was. There is cumulative force in these references. Elijah and the people of his time were not unacquainted with the facts recorded in the Books of Moses.

3. Going back to the Books of SAMUEL, we find Shiloh a *Quotations and references in Samuel.* centre of worship at the beginning (compare Josh. **18**. 1; Judg. **18**. 31). Hannah's words of thanksgiving show that she, at least, had learnt the old Memorial Song (compare 1 Sam. **2**. 2, 6 with Deut. **32**. 31, 39). The priestly system is recognized throughout the book—the sacrifices are going on, the fat is burnt, the Tabernacle of the Congregation is in use, the Ark of the Covenant of the Lord who dwelleth between the Cherubim, the Sabbath, the feast of the new moon, the yearly sacrifice, the shewbread, the ephod, the various methods of inquiring of the Lord by prophets, dreams, and Urim, are all well known.* We also find references to the plagues of Egypt (1 Sam. **4**. 8), to the hardening of Pharaoh's heart (**6**. 6), and to Rachel's sepulchre (**10**. 2).

In Samuel's speech (**12**. 6–17) we have an outline of the old Israelite history, including Jacob's entrance into Egypt, and the mission of Moses, Aaron, and some of the Judges. In chapter **15**, God reminds the people of what Amalek had done when Israel came out of Egypt. The case of Abimelech the son of Jerubbesheth, who died at Thebez, is cited by Joab, 2 Sam. **11**. 21.

4. What is the result so far attained? Is it not that from *Recapitulation.* the days of Samuel and onwards the people were in possession of the early books of our Bible? Are not there plain indications that the contents of the Pentateuch, Joshua, or the Judges were more or less known by the people? Does not the testimony so far imply that certain documents, answering in the main to these books as we now possess them, were in the safe keeping of those whose special duty it was to preserve them—*i.e.* the priestly families and other officials?

---

* It has been objected that sin-offerings are not noticed in the days of Samuel. But let the reader consider Lev. **10**. 16-20, and ask himself whether it is probable, or even possible, that the story of Moses' search for the sin-offering, his anger against Aaron, and his subsequent acceptance of Aaron's explanation, was an invention of later days.

Quotations and references in the Judges.

5. We now go back to the Book of JUDGES, which we take to be the work of the writers in the age of the earliest kings, and to be based on older documents, mainly contemporary with the events recorded. It contains twenty-one chapters, which cover a period of about four centuries, and it supplies full pictorial narratives of a few events threaded together on a very slight chronological system. We must not expect too much under these circumstances. The book hangs upon Joshua, just as the Books of Kings hang upon those of Samuel, taking up the history were the preceding book stops. After formally referring to Joshua's death, it freely refers to things recorded both in the preceding book and in the Pentateuch. It has already been pointed out that some portions of the first two chapters of the Judges are borrowed *verbatim* from Joshua **15, 16, 17,** and **24.** If the book contained no other evidence this would be considered sufficient, unless there were overwhelming reasons to the contrary, to justify us in affirming that the Book of Judges presupposes not only the facts recorded in Joshua, but the book itself. *See* Appendix, p. 203, for the chief parallel passages.

But there are other connecting links between the Judges and the older books ; examine, *e.g.*, the references to Moses' father-in-law (chap. **1.** 16 ; **4.** 11), the gift of Hebron to Caleb by Moses (**1.** 20 ; compare Deut. **1.** 36), God's oath to the Patriarchs concerning the land (**2.** 1), the penalties consequent on idolatry (**2.** 11–15, compare Lev. **26** and Deut. **28**), and God's repentance on the sight of their trouble (**2.** 18 ; compare Deut. **32.** 36). There are frequent references to Egyptian bondage and to the miracles connected with the Exodus (*e.g.* **6.** 8–13), whilst Jephthah's speech refers to Israel's early successes (**11.** 14–24). Nor must we omit to notice the casual reference to " the plain [or rather ' oak '] of the pillar in Shechem " (compare **9.** 6 with Josh. **24.** 26).

The precious words uttered to Gideon (**6.** 16), " Certainly I will be with thee," are an echo of the promise made under similar circumstances by God to Moses (Exod. **3.** 12). The request of Manoah to know the name of the angel of the Lord (**13.** 18) is answered in terms which bear a marked resemblance to those which we find in Gen. **32.** 29.

The Book of Judges is military rather than civil in its character. We should hardly expect to find in it any records of the Levitical ritual. There are, indeed, indications that there was such ritual. Thus, in chap. **20.** 27 we read of the Ark of the Covenant, and Phinehas the son of Eleazar, the son of Aaron, is described as standing before the Lord (compare Josh. **24.** 33). The reference to the Nazarite vow is also to be noticed (compare **13.** 4, 5 with Num. **6.** 2-8).

Bearing in mind the nature of the book and of its contents, and the strong reasons already pointed out for believing that the prophet Samuel and the men of his age knew the earlier books, we ask, is there or is there not sufficient evidence in the Book of Judges that it was preceded by some such events and institutions as are described in the first six books of the Old Testament? The evidence is slender, we must confess, and we should be glad to have more; but what there is must take its stand alongside of that we find in the Book of Samuel, and on the whole it seems to be sufficient.

CHAPTER IX.

THE CASE OF JOSHUA AND THE PENTATEUCH.

Interlocking of the first six books.

1. The relationship between the Book of JOSHUA and the PENTATEUCH is so marked that it is the habit of some critics to regard them as one compilation, and to call them "the Hexateuch." The Book of Joshua may certainly be regarded as a continuation of the Pentateuch, but it is by another hand. It implies the pre-existence of the earlier books throughout. Its theology and history are the outcome of the revelations and promises contained in the Pentateuch, and the references are too numerous and well-defined to be ignored.

These six books are a growth. The earlier elements reappear in the later developments of history, promise, and intervention. We may illustrate this from the first chapter of Genesis. The account of the making of man in the image of God (verse 27) is not only referred to in chap. **9. 6,** but is quoted *verbatim* in chap. **5. 1, 2.** The Sabbath rest (**2. 2**) is the basis of the Fourth Commandment (Exod. **20. 11**). The Garden of Eden (**2. 8**) is regarded as the perfection of beauty, and is referred to in this sense in chap. **13. 10.** The curse on the ground (**3. 17**) is reported to have been known by Lamech (**5. 29**), and is cited in the covenant made with Noah (**8. 21**). The blessing promised to Abraham and his seed (**12. 2,** &c.) appears to have been known to Balaam (Num. **24. 9**). The covenant concerning the land (**15. 18; 17. 7, 8**) and the oath which God sware to Abraham (**22. 15–18**) are not only referred to through the rest of the Patriarchal period, but form the basis of the series of interventions which spring therefrom. See, for example, Exod. **2. 24,** "God heard their groaning, and God remembered His covenant with Abraham, with Isaac, and with Jacob"; and compare Deut. **7. 7, 8,** "Because the

Lord loved you, and because He would keep the oath which He sware unto your fathers, hath the Lord brought you out," &c. The passages of this class are legion. One might as well stand on London Bridge and affirm that the Thames does not flow from above, as suggest that the dealings of God with Israel did not spring from the promises made in Patriarchal times and recorded in Genesis.

The overthrow of Sodom (Gen. **19.** 24, 25) is fully referred to in Deut. **29.** 23, some peculiar expressions specially linking the passages together, as we shall see later. The purchase of Machpelah by Abraham (chap. **23**) is referred to long afterwards in the parting instructions of Jacob (**49.** 29–32). The violent deeds of Simeon and Levi (**34.** 25, &c.) and the sin of Reuben (**35.** 22) are not only faithfully recorded in their place, but are remembered in later years and incorporated in Jacob's dying utterances concerning his sons. It is inconceivable that either the earlier record or the later utterance could have been invented in later days. The purchase of an estate by Jacob from the sons of Hamor (Gen. **33.** 19) is referred to by the writer of the last part of Joshua (**24.** 32), and the price paid, the terminology of which is peculiar, is specified in the latter as in the former passage.

2. The "bones of Joseph" (*i.e.* his mummy) may be called the material connecting link between the Patriarchal history contained in Genesis and the Israelite history which begins in Exodus (see Exod. **13.** 19, and compare Gen. **50.** 25 ; see also Heb. **11.** 22). The God of the Exodus is the God of Abraham, and the God of Isaac, and the God of Jacob, the same ever-living, ever-present, covenant-keeping God. His name JEHOVAH now became "known" in the fulness of its meaning. This could not have been the case until the promises made to the Patriarchs were fulfilled hundreds of years afterwards in the multiplication of Israel, in their redemption from Egypt, in the judgment on Egypt, and in the possession of the inheritance of Canaan (see Gen. **15.** 13–16). There is the same sort of relationship between

Exodus related to the later books.

Genesis and the rest of the Pentateuch that there is between the Old Testament and the New. One is the book
of Promise, the other is the book of Performance.

The "mixed multitude" (Exod. **12**. 38) reappear in
Numbers (**11**. 4), though the Hebrew words used are not
the same. The manna first mentioned in Exod. **16** is referred to in Num. **11** as causing dissatisfaction; and there
are verbal links between the passages. It reappears in
Moses' speeches (*e.g.* Deut. **8**. 3, 16), and the reason which
led God to bestow it is so important that it afterwards
became a shield in the hand of the Lord Jesus against
the fiery dart of Satan (see Matt. **4**. 4). The record of
the cessation of manna is recorded as a matter of history
in Josh. **5**. 12.

Further re-
lationships. 3. What need be added? Time would fail were we to
attempt a full and detailed account of the relationship,
theological, historical, legislative, and linguistic, between the
various parts of the Pentateuch. Let the student, instead
of beginning by noticing apparent inconsistencies, begin,
as must be accounted the fair critical method, by observing
and marking the points of connection, the coincidences,
designed and undesigned, between the books. Let him
notice, for example, how the attributes of God enumerated
formally in Exod. **34** are boldly cited by Moses in Num. **14**;
how the warning voice of Lev. **26** is heard again in
Deut. **28**; how the blessing of the tribes in Gen. **49** is
delicately linked with that contained in Deut. **33**; how
the history and legislation primarily affecting the people
who were brought out of Egypt are detailed in their leading outline in the addresses which were given by the aged
leaders to the next generation, and which bear the same sort
of relation to the earlier history as the Epistles of St. Paul
do to the Acts of the Apostles; how the references to
Joshua in the Pentateuch fit in with the full account of
his proceedings recorded in the book which bears his name;
how Phinehas, who was the priest when some of the events

mentioned in the Book of Judges took place, is referred to, almost casually, as coming to the front when his father succeeded to the priesthood (see Num. **25.** 10; **31.** 6).

4. Lastly, attention may be called to one small incident. *The brazen serpent.* We read in 2 Kings **18.**4, that Hezekiah broke in pieces the brazen serpent which Moses had made. Why did Moses make it? Where had it been kept? Why had it not been mentioned between the time of Moses and that of Hezekiah? The first question is easy to answer in the light of Num. **21.** 9. The second cannot be answered; but the fact remains that, just as the bones of Joseph linked the departure of Israel out of Egypt with the whole of the Patriarchal history, so this brazen serpent was a material link between the days when Israel was knocking at the door of Canaan and the times of Hezekiah. And what shall we say to the third question? Simply that there was no reason why it should have been mentioned in the intervening period. The argument from silence is a perilous one. This serpent was a "relic" for seven centuries, yet it was never referred to. Suddenly we learn that it had become the object of superstitious adoration, so it is destroyed. Even if the Law of Moses had never been referred to between the time of Joshua and that of Josiah, it might yet have been in existence. But with the facts before us which have been now brought out, every shadow of doubt must disappear. If there can be any stability in historical literature which is debarred through its antiquity from confirmation from external sources, we have got it in the precious documents which we have been examining in these three chapters.

CHAPTER X.

NOTES INTRODUCED INTO THE EARLY BOOKS.

Notes and parentheses. 1. No attentive reader of the Historical Books of the Old Testament can fail to observe that they contain a considerable number of notes. These notes are not printed as such in our Bibles, nor are they marked in any special way in the Hebrew MSS., but most of them can be detected without any such help, because they are all manifestly interruptions in the course of the narrative. We have, however, to draw a distinction at the outset between parentheses, which may have been the work of the original writers, and annotations, which have been added by later compilers and editors; though it may not always be clear to which class certain passages belong.

Gen. 2. 10-14. 2. An instance of a parenthesis rather than a note may be given, in the first place. In the second of Genesis, we have an account of the four rivers which started from the great watershed in which our first parents are reported to have lived. A description is given of the course of three of the rivers, but not of the fourth, which is supposed to be well known to the reader. If the description is part of the original document, we are evidently led to the conclusion that the writer lived near the Euphrates; and that seems the natural conclusion. At any rate, the earliest readers of the document must have lived in the Euphrates valley, for even the Hiddekel (*i.e.* the Tigris) needed a word of explanation.

Gen. 11. 3. In Gen. 11. 3 we find a note which cannot spring from a writer on the Euphrates. We read, "They had brick for stone, and slime had they for mortar." These words must have been written in a land where stone and mortar were in common use, and where brick and slime were comparatively rare. Can there be any doubt as to the birthplace of this note? Babylon is the land of brick, baked or sunburnt; whereas comparatively few bricks are to be seen in Palestine, which is a land of limestone. The piece of clay ground near Zaretan, in which Solomon's castings were prepared, seems to have been regarded as quite a rarity (see 1 Kings 7. 42; 2 Chron. 4. 17). What clay there was in the land was chiefly needed for making pottery, and it is thought from the name (חמר) to have been of reddish tint, though this is doubtful. The clay from which the old Babylonian bricks are made is a yellowish white, and the name of a brick (לבנה) indicates its colour. This same name is given to the blackish bricks of Egypt in the Book of Exodus—a clear proof that the name had originated in the Babylonian region, had travelled with the Patriarchs to Canaan, and had gone on with them to Egypt, where it had to do duty for a very different-looking material. It may seem strange to us, who live in a land rich in brick and mortar, that after the Exodus bricks are not so much as named in the Bible till the days of Isaiah, though a brick-kiln, or, as we might translate it, bakery, is mentioned in 2 Sam. 12. 31.

Passing on to Gen. 12. 6, and 13. 7, we have short parenthetic notes—" The Canaanite was then in the land," and " The Canaanite and the Perizzite dwelled then in the land." *Gen. 12. 6. and 13. 7.* These words would hardly be part of the original record kept by the Patriarchs. Who wrote them? and with what object? The first of them gives force to the great promise introduced in the next verse—" Unto thy seed will I give this land "; and the other adds point to the offer made by Abraham to Lot—" Is not the whole land before thee? " Whoever it was that welded the original records into one continuous narrative may well have inserted these words, or they may have been added by a later hand.

We have found a Euphratean note and a Canaanite note; *Gen. 13. 10.* let us now look at an Egyptian note. In Gen. 13. 10 we are told that " Lot lifted up his eyes, and saw the plain of

Jordan, that it was well watered everywhere, before the Lord overthrew Sodom and Gomorrah, even as the garden of the Lord, like the land of Egypt, as thou comest unto Zoar." First we have the fact, recorded at the time, that Lot viewed the plain or 'Arabah of the Jordan; secondly, the compiler's note that it was a well-watered region before the overthrow; thirdly, there is a comparison with the garden of the Lord, and so we have a reminiscence of Eden, which seems to have been the standard of perfection in old times (compare Isa. **51**. 3—"He will make her wilderness like Eden, and her desert like the garden of the Lord"; so Joel **2**. 3, and Ezek. **28**. 13; and compare the old Babylonian expression *Gan-Dunia*); fourthly, the region is compared with the land of Egypt, *i.e.* the well-watered territory of Goshen, especially its eastern part. It has been pointed out by the Rev. H. Tompkins that the word written "Zoar" may have been Zar or Zal, the north-eastern boundary of Egypt, where it joins the Philistine territory. Others think that the word was originally written *Zoan*. At any rate, this description looks as if it came from the hand of Moses, and was an illustration designed for the benefit of his contemporaries, who knew Egypt but not Sodom.

Gen. 14. The 14th of Genesis contains a series of topographical notes, evidently not part of the original document, but proceeding from a later hand. Thus we have Bela, which is Zoar (verse 2); the vale of Siddim, which is the Salt Sea (verse 3); En-mishpat, which is Kadesh (verse 7); Hobah, which is on the left of Damascus (verse 15); the valley of Shaveh, which is the King's dale (verse 17). These notes look as if they were written for the benefit of Israel after they had settled in Canaan. In each case the old name had passed away, and a descriptive note was needed. If we could tell the date of any of the later expressions we might get a key to the age of the annotator; but any one of them might have been written by Moses, though they are probably later. The "King's dale" is referred to in 2 Sam. **18**. 18, as containing Absalom's pillar, but the dale probably received its name from the fact that it was the meeting-place between the king of Sodom, Abraham, and Melchizedek.

Gen. **26.** 1 reads thus—" And there was a famine in the *Gen.* 26. 1. land, beside the first famine that was in the days of Abraham." The last clause seems to be an explanatory note by the compiler—whom we take to be Moses—to prevent any confusion as to the two famines. There are similar explanatory expressions running through the books, but it is not easy to tell how many of them are part of the original history, and how many are the work of a subsequent annotator.

Part of Gen. **36.** 31 must have been a late addition ; that *Gen.* 36. 31– is to say, it could not have been included in its present form ³⁰. in the documents which had passed, through Joseph, into the hands of Moses. It seems impossible that Moses could have found or written the words—" These are the kings that reigned in the land of Edom *before there reigned any king over the children of Israel."* The words in italics cannot well have been added till the time of Samuel. It is to be noticed that the chronicler extracted the whole passage with these words in it (1 Chron. **1.** 43), so that the chapter in Genesis must have stood in his time very much as it stands now.

We pass on now to Gen. **43.** 32, where we have an ex- *Gen.* 43. 32. planatory note of considerable importance. A separate table was prepared for the Hebrews "because the Egyptians might not eat bread with the Hebrews, for that is an abomination unto the Egyptians." It is usual to connect this passage with the fact that the Egyptians were at this time under the dominion of the Shepherd kings, but this is uncertain, though highly probable. A somewhat similar note is to be found in Gen. **46.** 34, where we are told that every shepherd is an abomination unto the Egyptians. On turning to Exod. **8.** 26 we read concerning the victims of sacrifice that "they are the abomination of the Egyptians"; and here we probably get the key to the earlier annotation. Moses evidently used the word "abomina-

tion " (תועבה) in Deut. **7.** 25 and other passages for an
idol, or something hateful to God, and to be avoided by
Israel. We may therefore gather that what was sacred to
the Egyptians in connection with their idolatrous rites was
hateful in the sight of God. The Egyptians did not hate
sheep and oxen; they deified the bull; and this superstition
was an abomination to the Lord. So it may be that the
shepherds and the Hebrews (who were evidently identified
with shepherds) were not hated by the Egyptians, but their
calling was connected with certain rites which were sacred
to them, and to be abominated by the Israelites. Perhaps
they were tabooed. It would not be safe to indicate any
relationship between the South Sea Taboo and the word
Toabah, which we translate abomination, but the one custom
may possibly illustrate the other. Whatever interpretation
we give to the note, it cannot well be brought down to a
later time than that of Moses. .

Exod. 16. 35. 3. In Exod. **16.** 35 we are told that Israel ate the manna
forty years, until they came to a land inhabited; they did
eat manna until they came unto the borders of the land of
Canaan. This is evidently a note added after the event, and
probably by the compiler of the Book of Joshua (compare
Josh. **5.** 12). The next verse contains a note also, to show
the proportion which an omer bears to an ephah. There
are other notes bearing on weights and measures, which we
may have to refer to later on.

Num. 13. 22. 4. In Num. **13.** 22 the spies are said to have ascended
by the south and come to Hebron, and it is added, "Now
Hebron was built seven years before Zoan in Egypt." This
refers to a very ancient piece of history indeed. Zoan is
old, but Hebron is seven years older. Why should Zoan,
of all places, be taken as a standard of antiquity? The
answer is an interesting one. Zoan had not been so much
as named before, and yet every Israelite knew it, for it was
a sort of metropolis to Goshen, and it is here and in the
neighbourhood that the mighty works of God had been done

(see Ps. **78**. 12, 43). Moses may well have known the age of Zoan; but who knew the age of Hebron? That must have been learnt on the spot or in the neighbourhood. Thus this little note must have proceeded from one who knew personally or by hearsay concerning the respective ages of Zoan and Hebron. Was it Moses? Was it Joshua or Caleb? Or was it Phinehas? We cannot well go later than their time. In any case, the "building" may not have been the first settlement of the place, but its establishment as a walled city, as in other passages.

The note on the character of Moses (Num. **12**. 3) was, of *Num.* 12. 3. course, not written by himself; at least, it is not likely that he would write it; yet it bears the marks of a contemporary writer or of a very early annotator, and would be of the age of the preceding one.

In Num. **32**. 41 we read that Jair the son of Manasseh *Num.* 32. 41. went and took the small towns of Gilead, and called them Havoth-jair. It is generally supposed that this must have been inserted in later times, and it may have been so. We have it again in a corresponding passage (Deut. **3**. 14), with rather fuller particulars; also in Josh. **13**. 10. It appears again in 1 Chron. **2**. 22, where we find that Jair was the descendant of Segub, who sprang from Judah on his father's side, and from Gilead the Manassite on his mother's side, and that the villages or towns were sixty in number. So far there is no difficulty in ascribing the passages in Numbers and Deuteronomy to the age of Moses. But apparently Jair lived some time afterwards, for in Judges **10**. 3, 4 he is introduced as judging Israel after the period of Abimelech —"And he had thirty sons, and they had thirty cities, which are called Havoth-jair (*i.e.* towns of Jair) unto this day." Were there two Gileadite Jairs, one in the age of Joshua, and one considerably later? This is quite possible. Did the first call a group of villages Havoth-jair, and did the second revive the name owing to the fact that he had sway over part of his ancestor's territory, and was rich in sons? We see no difficulty in this supposition.

5. In the second and third chapters of Deuteronomy there are some important parentheses of an ethnological character which call for attention. Moses is reviewing the history of the past, and after describing the compassing of Mount Seir "many days" (*i.e.* thirty-eight years) proceeds to speak of Moab. Then comes a note on the original inhabitants of these regions, viz., the Horim of Seir and the Emim of Moab (2. 10–12). The aborigines of the Ammonite and Philistine territories, viz., the Zamzummim and the Avim, are mentioned just below (verses 20–23). If these passages were not part of the original speech they must be very ancient notes. There seems no reason for bringing them lower than the age of Phinehas. The reference to Og's bedstead of iron (? basalt) in chap. 3. 11 is probably a note, and so is the ninth verse, which gives the Amorite and Sidonian ways of spelling the old name of Hermon.

There are short historical parentheses in these old speeches which form quite a peculiar feature in them; see, for example, the severance of the refuge cities (4. 41–13); the reference to the sins committed at Taberah, Massah, and other places (9. 22–24); also, a section of the journeyings (10. 6, 7) taken from Num. 33. 30–33. The first and third of these passages look to us like intrusions on the text, but they may have been inserted by the original compiler of the book in the days of Joshua. The last sentences of the book tell us that there arose not a prophet since in Israel like unto Moses. This must be a reflection on the part of a historian of later times. It can hardly have been written before the age of Samuel, and it may well have been later. The words seem to have special reference to the promise in the 18th chapter, where provision was made for the future raising up of a prophet like unto Moses.

6. Most of the notes referred to above are of an archæological or historical character. But our attention is now called to a comment on the text which is of the nature of a theological reflection. In Josh. 11. 20, after referring to

Joshua's annexation of all the Canaanite territories except
that of the Hivites of Gibeon, the writer adds—"For it was
of the Lord to harden their hearts that they should come
against Israel in battle that he might destroy them utterly."
Compare with this the comment on Samson's case in
Judg. **14.** 4—"His father and his mother knew not that
it was of the Lord that he sought an occasion against the
Philistines"; also 1 Sam. **2.** 25, where we are told that the
sons of Eli "hearkened not unto the voice of their father
because the Lord would slay them," and 2 Sam. **17.** 14—
"For the Lord had appointed to defeat the good counsel
of Ahithophel, to the intent that the Lord might bring evil
upon Absalom." This last passage is part of the work of
either Nathan or Gad, and there seems considerable likeli-
hood that these writers, in conjunction with their elder
coadjutor Samuel, would review the writings of the past,
and that they, under Divine guidance, might point to the
hand of Providence in the previous history of their people,
by some such comments as we have called attention to. To
them also, or to the prophetic scribes of a later day, might
be attributed such a reflection as we find recorded in Josh.
10. 14—"There was no day like that before it or *after it*,
that the Lord hearkened unto the voice of a man."

7. In the later chapters of the Judges we are introduced *Judg.* 18. 30.
to a very ancient series of historical events which might well
be placed much earlier in the book. In the course of the
narrative we are told (**18.** 30) that certain persons were
"priests to the tribe of Dan until the day of the captivity of
the land." This is manifestly a note; but what is its date?
The word translated "captivity" (גלה) is used here in this
sense for the first time. It is one of many words which have
a double significance, being sometimes used of "uncovering"
in the sense of "revelation," and sometimes of "stripping"
or "carrying captive." The next place where it is used is
in connection with the ark in 1 Sam. **4.** 21, 22, where we
read that the glory is "departed"—taken captive—from

Israel. The well-known incident is referred to in Ps. 78. 59–61, where we read that God was provoked with the graven images and high places of Israel—

> So that He forsook the tabernacle of Shiloh,
> The tent which He placed among men ;
> And delivered His strength into captivity,
> And His glory into the enemy's hand.

Some critics consider that "the captivity of the land" was the great stripping and desolation of the land under the iron rule of Philistia. It might well be so described, even if we declined to follow the suggestion of some that the word "land" (אֶרֶץ) is a misreading for "ark" (אֲרוֹן). One sees no reason, however, why the semi-idolatrous priesthood over Dan should be affected by the Philistine tyranny. The probabilities are rather in favour of the note being added by a later historian. · The fact might well have been recorded in the age of Hezekiah, who, as we know, sent commissioners through all the tribes of Israel as far north as Dan (see 2 Chron. 30).

CHAPTER XI.

OTHER NOTES IN THE HISTORICAL BOOKS.

1. There is a brief note frequently to be found in the *"Unto this day."* Historical Books of the Old Testament to which we must now call attention. Some event, custom, or local object is spoken of as remaining up to the time of the writer, *i.e.* the annotator or compiler. The first time these words occur is with respect to the origin of Moab and Ammon, who were the fathers of the Moabites and of the children of Ammon "unto this day."

2. Some of these notes bear on the origin of well-known *Archaic names.* local names. Thus, after the oath made between Isaac and the officers of Abimelech (itself a renewal of a more ancient agreement, as may be seen by comparing Gen. **21.** 31 with chap. **26.** 33), we read, " Therefore the name of the city is Beer-sheba unto this day." Similar local notes will be found on Succoth (Gen. **33.** 17), Abel-mizraim, which is beyond Jordan (Gen. **50.** 11), Havoth-jair (Deut **3.** 14), Gilgal (Josh. **5.** 9), the valley of Achor (Josh. **7.** 26), Luz (Judg. **1.** 26), En-hakkore (Judg. **15.** 19), Mahaneh-Dan (Judg. **18.** 12), Perez-uzzah (2 Sam. **6.** 8), Absalom's place (2 Sam. **18.** 18).

3. Others relate to the permanence of old customs, the *Ancient customs.* origin of which has been described in the text. Thus, in Gen. **32.** 32 we read, " Therefore the children of Israel eat not of the sinew which shrank, which is upon the hollow of the thigh, unto this day." This is the first appearance of the familiar expression " the children of Israel," or, as an Oriental would say, Beni-Israel. The note might have been inserted at any time, for the custom is even now prevalent among strict Jews. Again, in Gen. **47.** 26, we are told that

"Joseph made it a law over the land of Egypt unto this day, that Pharaoh should have the fifth part." Was this a Mosaic note? or was it the testimony of much later times? Both of these notes may have proceeded from Moses.

In Josh. 9. 27 Joshua is said to have "made (or appointed) the Gibeonites to be hewers of wood and drawers of water for the congregation, and for the altar of the Lord, even unto this day, in the place which he should choose." It is generally believed that these Gibeonites were the people afterwards called Nethinim, of whom we read (Ezra 8. 20) that David and the princes had appointed them for the service of the Levites. The word Nethinim is one of several words peculiar to Chronicles, Ezra, and Nehemiah, and is derived from the word נתן (*nathan*) translated "made" in the verse quoted above from Joshua. The Gibeonites held a special position "by appointment," and whilst they on their part were bound to render yeoman's service, Israel was bound to protect them, as Saul's family found to their cost (see the parenthesis in 2 Sam. 21. 2). It may be that David, amongst his other labours, reviewed the position of these Gibeonites and renewed the covenant made with them. In the days of Nehemiah they had their own chief, and a locality on Ophel was assigned to them (Neh. 11. 21).

In 1 Sam. 5. 5 we are told that the priests of Dagon do not tread on the threshold of Dagon in Ashdod "unto this day." Some think that this custom is referred to in Zeph. 1. 9, but this is very doubtful. There were Ashdodites in the days of Nehemiah, and the note may have been added at any time. In 1 Sam. 30. 25 David is said to have made a certain ordinance concerning the division of spoil "unto this day." This note may be of any age, but the note on 1 Sam. 27. 6 (Ziklag pertaineth unto the kings of Judah unto this day) can hardly have been written later than the Captivity. It looks more like a note of the age of Hezekiah, as may have been the case with the two preceding. The last words of 2 Sam. 5. 8 may be a note, but their meaning is not quite certain.

4. Other notes of a historical or local character may be *Historical notes.* grouped together. Thus, Hebron became the inheritance of Caleb unto this day (Josh. **14.** 14); the Geshurites and the Maachathites dwell among the Israelites unto this day (Josh. **13.** 13)—hence the connection of both with David (2 Sam. **3.** 3); the Jebusites dwell with the children of Judah at Jerusalem unto this day (Josh. **15.** 63); the Canaanites dwell among the Ephraimites unto this day, and serve under tribute (Josh. **16.** 10). With these passages may be compared 1 Kings **9.** 21, "All the people left of the Amorites, Hittites, Perizzites, Hivites, and Jebusites . . . upon those did Solomon levy a tribute of bondservice unto this day." Hence they were called "the children of Solomon's servants" (Ezra **2.** 55). Many of them went into captivity, and many of them came out again. These notes may have been as late as Nehemiah's time, though, of course, they may have been of Hezekiah's time. A note of a similar character, relating to the Beerothites, is to be found in 2 Sam. **4.** 3.

In 2 Kings **8.** 22 we read that Edom revolted from under the hand of Judah unto this day; and in chap. **16.** 6 the Syrians are said to have come to Elath and dwelt there unto this day. In 1 Chron. **5.** 22 the Reubenites and others are described as conquering the Hagarites and dwelling in their steads "until the Captivity"; whilst immediately below, Pul and Tiglath-pileser are said to have carried away the two and a half tribes, and settled them elsewhere "unto this day." These notes may also date from the age of Hezekiah.

In the case of Simeon's descendants (1 Chron. **4.** 41, 43) we read of certain movements which happened in the days of Hezekiah, in consequence of which the Hamites and Amalekites were dispossessed unto this day. These may be the chronicler's own notes, or they may have been copied by him from earlier documents, as in the case of several extracts from Kings, where the expression "there they are unto this day," or some kindred expression, was mechanically repeated

by the recorder, even when inapplicable to his own time.
See, for instances, 1 Chron. **13.** 11; 2 Chron. **5.** 9 (with
reference to the ark); **10.** 19; **21.** 10.

Only one other note which strictly belongs to this class
need be mentioned, viz., 2 Kings **17.** 34, 41. It has to do
with the ways of the people who were introduced into the
land of Israel by the Assyrian conquerors. "Unto this
day," says the writer, "they do after the former manners . . .
as did their fathers, so do they unto this day." This para-
graph might have been written by Jeremiah, whom we take
to be the last substantial contributor to the Kings; but it
may have been of the post-Captivity period, when the line
of religious demarcation between Samaria and Judah was
so strongly emphasized.

*Monumen-
tal notes.*

5. Another class of notes refers to certain monuments still
existing in the time of the annotator. Thus, the twelve
stones put by Joshua in the midst of Jordan are there unto
this day (Josh. **4.** 9). Ai stands as a heap (still called Et-
Tell, "the heap") unto this day, and a cairn or heap of
stones raised over the king's dead body remaineth unto this
day (Josh. **8.** 28). The great stones remain at the mouth
of the cave of Makkedah unto this day (Josh. **10.** 27), and
the stone of Abel is said to remain on the estate of the Beth-
shemite unto this day (1 Sam. **6.** 18); also the temple of
Baal at Samaria was made a draught-house by Jehu unto
this day (2 Kings **10.** 27). None of these notes are likely
to have been latter than the Captivity, and it would appear
probable that they were of the age of Hezekiah, in whose
time there may also have been added such notes as we find
in 1 Kings **8.** 8, on the staves; in chap. **12.** 19, on the
secession; in 2 Kings **2.** 22, on the fountain of Jericho;
in chap. **8.** 22, on Edom; in chap. **14.** 7, on Joktheel; and
in chap. **16.** 6, on Elath.

*Literary
notes.*

6. Another class of notes may be called literary. They
record sayings, or give a reference to some writing. Thus,

in Gen. **22.** 14 we read, "Abraham called the name of that place Jehovah-jireh [the Lord will provide], as it is said to this day, In the mountain of the Lord it shall be provided." Here was a strange saying with reference to "the mountain of the Lord." Can there be any doubt as to the locality of the mountain, or as to the spirit of the saying? It is almost a prophecy of "the great provision." The two references to the Book of Jasher would come under this head (Josh. **10.** 13; 2 Sam. **1.** 18); also the reference to the Book of the Wars of the Lord (Num. **21.** 14), and to them "that speak in proverbs" (verse 27). In 1 Sam. **9.** 9 we have the noteworthy remark on the change of the word "seer" to the later form "prophet," and in chap. **10.** 12 we are told that it became a proverbial expression (as it is still) to say, Is Saul also among the prophets? (Compare chap. **19.** 23, 24.) With these we may put the reference to the lamentations made over Josiah in 2 Chron. **34.** 25.

7. The only other notes to which we have to call attention are the archæological comments on names. Many Biblical names of places are more or less monumental in their character, and they originated in various ways. There were the old Canaanitish names, which were changed to a considerable extent when Israel entered upon their inheritance. There were names which originated in the family names of the possessors of various estates. Some were descriptive, such as the Carmels, the Jeshimons, the Gibeahs or Gebahs, and the Ramahs. Others were derived from certain events in the Patriarchal or later ages, many of these being connected with supernatural or providential circumstances. We have already called attention to the notes on the names in Gen. **14.** Let us look at a few more of the same class.

Explanations of local names.

Gen. **13.** 18, Abram dwelt in the plain of Mamre (which is in Hebron); chap. **16.** 14, Wherefore the well was called Beer-lahai-roi (behold, it is between Kadesh and Bered)— was not this note written by Moses in the wilderness?

—chap. **19**. 20, 22, Behold now, this city is near to flee unto, and it is a little one. . . . Therefore the name of the city was called Zoar; chap. **23**. 2, 19, Sarah died in Kirjath-arba (the same is Hebron in the land of Canaan); chap. **28**. 19, Jacob called the name of that place Bethel (but the name of that city was Luz at the first); chap. **35**. 19, Ephrath (which is Bethlehem).

A later series of the same character are to be found in Joshua and Judges. Thus, Josh. **15**. 8, The south side of the Jebusite (the same is Jerusalem); verse 9, Baalah (which is Kirjath-jearim); verse 15, And he went up to the inhabitants of Debir (and the name of Debir before was Kirjath-sepher); verse 25, Hezron (which is Hazor); chap. **18**. 13, Luz (which is Bethel); verse 28, Jebusi (which is Jerusalem); chap. **20**. 7, They appointed Kedesh in Galilee (in Mount Naphtali), and Shechem (in Mount Ephraim), and Kirjath-arba (which is Hebron).

A few notes from Judges may be added. Chap. **1**. 10, Now the name of Hebron before was Kirjath-arba; chap. **6**. 24, Then Gideon built an altar there unto the Lord, and called it Jehovah-shalom (unto this day it is yet in Ophrah of the Abi-ezrites); chap. **7**. 1, Jerubbaal (who is Gideon)—compare Acts **13**. 9, " Saul, who is also called Paul"; chap. **15**. 19, He called the name thereof En-hakkore (which is in Lehi) unto this day; chap. **19**. 10, Jebus (which is Jerusalem); chap. **21**. 12, They brought them unto the camp to Shiloh (which is in the land of Canaan). This last seems the strangest of all notes, but the words must be read with their context. Jabesh-Gilead, from which the damsels were brought, was out of the land of Canaan; hence the reason and the force of the note. Compare similar cases in Gen. **33**. 18 ; **48**. 3 ; **49**. 30. Notes of this class get fewer as the reason for them diminishes. The case of Berachah in 2 Chron. **20**. 26 is one of the latest.

In 1 Sam. **23**. 28 we read, " Therefore they called that place Sela-hammahlekoth "; 2 Sam. **2**. 16, " Wherefore that place was called Helkath-hazzurim, which is in Gibeon ";

chap. **5**. 20, "Therefore he called the name of that place Baal-perazim." These are not necessarily notes by a later hand; they form part of the original document, and may be compared with Matt. **27**. 8, where we are told that the field was called the field of blood "unto this day," *i.e.* till the time when the Gospel was written.

In 2 Sam. **5**. 6 we are told that the king went to Jerusalem. The chronicler in extracting the passage adds, "which is Jebus" (1 Chron. **11**. 4). Why did he add this? It seems to be a final record of the old name before it passed away for ever. Thus, whilst in the earlier books we have "Jebus, which is Jerusalem," in the later we have "Jerusalem, which is Jebus." The change is significant. The ancient name of Kirjath-jearim (viz., Baalah) is still preserved with its more modern representative in 1 Chron. **13**. 6, just as the parallel names "the city of David, which is Zion," stand together in 2 Chron. **5**. 2. Compare also the names Hazezon-Tamar and Engedi (chap. **20**. 2).

8. It is time now to draw this somewhat minute branch of *Summary.* our discussion to a close. It is the duty of critics to look into these things, and it demands patience, attention, and honesty, especially when we seek to draw conclusions. Still the conclusions in this case are very clear. We find many archæological, explanatory, and illustrative notes in the earlier books, and few in the later. By far the most are in the books which profess to be the oldest. The notes themselves are ancient, and they throw back the text into far more ancient times. None of the notes seem later than Nehemiah's time; many are before the Captivity. Some of these are from the hand of Moses; others, probably, from Phinehas, Samuel, the prophets of Hezekiah's age (*e.g.* Isaiah), and Jeremiah. Those in the Pentateuch must probably have been introduced before it was written in the roll-form. They are all silent witnesses to the antiquity of the text on which they comment.

F

CHAPTER XII.

FIDELITY OF THE WRITERS AND COMPILERS.

Questions concerning editorship. 1. We now go back from the ancient notes to the still more ancient substance of the Historical Books, which we regard as having been compiled by a succession of prophetic men from the age of Moses to that of Nehemiah. Fresh questions now present themselves for discussion. We ask, for example, how far did the compilers feel themselves at liberty to "compound" their materials? Would Moses feel it his duty simply to string together the Patriarchal documents which fell into his hands when he took charge of the national archives, or would he allow himself to adjust them to one another by a certain amount of editorial work? We may safely reply that he would take the latter course. And if parallel accounts of some of the events had been handed down from primæval times, would he be justified in blending them into one narrative, as the chronicler did in later times? An affirmative answer may certainly be given to this question. Again, the oldest accounts of all would not be originally in Hebrew but in the pre-Babel tongue, or in some such language as the Accadian. In process of transmission some of the narratives might need to be translated. Who would be answerable for the fidelity of the translation? We should have to go back to the Patriarchal age for a reply. Once more, the original race must have had a common tradition, say, concerning the Creation, the Fall, and the Deluge; this tradition would assume a very different colouring amongst the various nationalities which sprang up after the scattering of mankind. Moses manifestly adopted the old Patriarchal or Euphratean tradition, though he must have been conscious that the Egyptians amongst whom he lived saw and taught things very differently. Probably the tendency to differentiation was much more strong, both in physiology and in literature, during the first ages than in after times. Another tendency subsequently set in, viz., in the direction of fixity, crystallization, or incrustation. This may account for many things which are at present a puzzle to us.

2. We must, however, assign limits to the editorial liberty *Fidelity of Moses.* assumed by Moses in preparing Genesis. If he had a conviction—and that he had is clearly to be shown from his recorded addresses—that the Genesis documents set forth the dealings and purposes and laws of the Living and True God, then we may be sure that he would regard the archives committed to him as a sacred trust; he would look upon them as the title-deeds of the nation and of the race; and he would respect their very letter to the uttermost, not tampering with their contents, but restricting what we moderns call editorial work to very narrow limits. He would, indeed, do what in him lay to make the records intelligible to the ordinary reader of his time, and to put them in chronological order; and if—which is quite possible—he had parallel accounts of some events, he would doubtless harmonize and combine them as best he could, looking upward to the ever-present God for guidance and direction. And when we thus speak of Moses, whom we have been led to consider the final authority, under God, for the earliest part of the Biblical literature, we include any persons whom he employed as scribes or copyists.

We should add that it would not be needful in Moses' time to translate out of Accadian or any other primæval language. This was already done, in the post-Babel age. Nor is there anything in Genesis which could not have come to Moses through Joseph's line, except the Edomite genealogy (Gen. **36**. 31, &c.), and some few ethnological particulars, which may have been appended in later times.

The fact that there is a gulf of above a century (to say the very least) between the end of Genesis and the beginning

F 2

of Exodus is no slight testimony to Moses' faithfulness in restricting himself to his plain duty as a conserver of the Patriarchal documents. It would have been so easy for him to give an account of the intermediate period, with stories of the Shepherd kings, and an account of the rise of the 18th Egyptian dynasty, together with details of the ways of the Egyptians, and the fortunes of the children of Israel. But he abstained, presenting thereby a favourable contrast with the late Jewish writer Josephus.

Another testimony to Moses' faithfulness is to be seen in the theology of his writings. The books which passed under his hands possess, indeed, a slight—a very slight—Egyptian colouring; but neither the Patriarchal narratives nor the beliefs impressed upon Israel savoured of Egyptianism. The stream of Truth which issued from the Euphrates valley and passed through Canaan made its way through the land of Egypt and the period of bondage absolutely untainted, so far as we can judge.

Moses thus set an example of literary fidelity which must have impressed itself upon his followers; and, without going further into details, we shall take it for granted that the prophetic compilers of later ages were not slow to follow his example. They did full justice to the materials which they had access to, reproducing them faithfully, modernizing their language where necessary, introducing notes to illustrate the older text, and blending parallel narratives into one account if they were fortunate enough to possess them.

Reports of speeches. 3. One of the peculiarities of the books which we are discussing is that they abound in speeches, dialogues, and conversations. Again and again the question rises in one's mind, How can these words have been reported? How did the sacred writer get hold of them? We doubt if any complete answer could be given to this inquiry. It would be an interesting problem to take the sacred history page by page and investigate the possible source of each narrative. But such a work, after all, would be an idle speculation, so much would be left to the imagination of the investigator. Can we, however, get any light on the matter?

We may divide the utterances in question into three *Messages from God.* classes. First come those which are professedly from God. We are told that God spoke to Moses face to face, as a man speaks to his friend (Exod. **33.** 11 ; Num. **12.** 8), whilst He spoke to prophets in a vision or a dream, presenting truth to the eye under symbols, or to the ear in articulate words, such as those which made Samuel run to Eli. Sometimes the Divine utterance seemed to come from heaven itself ; sometimes through the medium of an angel or spiritual messenger who might appear in human form. In these and kindred methods, it seemed good to the Most High to communicate with select members of the human family ; and we can readily understand that such communications would make a deep and abiding impression on the heart and memory of the favoured prophet, so that he would be able to reproduce them with great exactness, whether by word of mouth or in writing. The prophet Jeremiah was instructed to commit to writing all that God had spoken to him from the days of Josiah to the fourth year of Jehoiakim (Jer. **36.** 2), and it seems to have been no difficulty to him to do so. In the case of the legislative utterances, and the directions for the Tabernacle, which God is represented as making known to Moses, there seems to have been plenty of time allowed between one communication and another for the recording of the laws and regulations and ordinances which were to be afterwards promulgated. A series of visions indelibly impressed on the inner man during a period of forty days, with supplementary revelations in later times, would supply ample materials for the legislative and ceremonial parts of Exodus and Leviticus and Numbers.

So far there is really no difficulty, if we allow with all due reverence that the one living and true God, the Fountain of all human and superhuman wit and wisdom, has come into touch with mankind and has made known His will, not only in ordinary ways through the universal conscience and reason, but in special or extraordinary ways as well. He who is not prepared to allow this must deal with the phenomena presented in the manifestation of Jesus Christ, and with many other phenomena, before he can negative this preliminary position.

Let us say, then, that thanks to the peculiar nature of the impressions made by the Spirit of God on the spirit of man, we have an adequate and faithful representation in these books of certain utterances of God, *e.g.* the promises and threats made to Adam, Noah, Abraham, and other favoured individuals, through a course of many centuries. But these utterances have human surroundings; they are in a terrestrial framework. We have long *speeches*, *e.g.* those of Moses, of Joshua, of Jephthah, of Samuel, of the Wise Woman of Tekoah, of David; we have long *prayers*, *e.g.* those of Abraham's servant, and of Ezra; we have long *hymns*, *e.g.* those of Moses, of Hannah, of Deborah and Barak, of David; we have long *blessings*, *e.g.* of Jacob and of Moses. Are these trustworthy? We have already seen that the books are composed from contemporary sources, and by men who claim, and have a right to be, trusted. And so, whilst ready to admit that the invention of imaginary speeches is a very old art—much older than the days of Thucydides—we give the sacred writers the credit of reporting and not inventing these speeches and hymns. Many of the addresses in question, *e.g.* those of Moses and Jephthah, were of an official character, and in such cases the scribes and recorders of the day would be busy with their pens. Others, *e.g.* the utterances of Jacob on his deathbed, would be stamped upon the memory of the many hearers, all of whom were personally interested in what was said, and so they would be preserved from the day of their utterance. In other cases the tenor of the address may have been publicly known, and the speech, as we have it, would be a record of the substance of what was said.

Reports of conversations.   4. Again, there are endless varieties of conversation and dialogue—public, domestic, and private. These make up the

clothing of the bones of history, and add much to the fresh-
ness and vigour of the Bible. Have we any reason to doubt
the substantial accuracy of the record which contains them ?
Many of them must have been hearsay. But we are dealing
with the writings of the most gifted people in the world; we
are dealing with narratives indited by men whose memories
—much stronger by nature than ours—were stimulated and
quickened by a Power greater than their own ; we are dealing with men thus capable of working out what we should
call a hint, and of clothing passing events in appropriate
language. Thus we have before us in these endless bits of
conversation a picture of the things as they really happened.
Our faith does not hang on the recorded utterances of Sarah,
Leah, Reuben, Judah, Pharaoh, Jethro, Ahab, Jezebel, and
the rest ; but their utterances are related to the surrounding
history, and this we accept as true, and important to be
received and believed. The words and the deeds fit together ;
each helps us to understand the other ; all are links in a long
chain of history which is being slowly elaborated by an
unseen Hand ; and all are written for our instruction.

5. We cannot forget that the point now before us has an
important bearing on the composition of the New Testament. The Gospels and Acts are largely made up of conversations and addresses. Some of them were of a public
character; others were quite private. Who reported our
Lord's conversation with Nicodemus, or with the woman of
Samaria ? Who preserved to us the utterances of the priests
concerning the price of blood, or the conversation of Pilate
and our Lord in the Judgment-hall ? How did anyone get
hold of the chief captain's letter to Felix, or of the speech
made by the orator Tertullus ? We should have to put aside
many sections of the Gospels and Acts as hearsay or invention were it not for one thing. We believe the books to
have been the work of Apostles and Prophets ; we believe
that these Apostles and Prophets were under the all-sufficient
influence of the Holy Spirit, who brought all things to their

*Analogy of
the New
Testament.*

remembrance, guiding them into all truth, giving them access to all needful materials, and supplying them with the necessary skill and wisdom which should enable them to present the truth in suitable language. There may often have been persons listening to conversations whose presence is not referred to in Scripture. Some disciple, *e.g.* St. John, may have been present when our Lord talked with Nicodemus or the Samaritan woman. Officials, such as Cornelius, may have been in Pilate's company when he questioned the Lord. The letter of Lysias may have come from archives, or may have been read out in Paul's hearing. So also it may have been with regard to the numerous conversations and addresses in the Old Testament.

CHAPTER XIII.

SOME PECULIARITIES IN THE STYLE OF THE WRITERS.

1. We have been led to the conclusion that the substance *Was trans-*
of the early books is to a large extent preserved to us in the *lation neces-*
style and condition in which the original writers left it, and *sary?*
that this accounts for the presence of numerous comparatively late (though really ancient) notes which would not
have been needed if the materials had been largely remodelled
after the Captivity. It has also been pointed out that some
parts are presented in translations from foreign languages,
e.g. possibly some of the very earliest documents in
Genesis. The same is the case with some of the latest
decrees and letters in Ezra. An interesting illustration of
this process may be seen elsewhere; for students of Assyrian tell us that numerous tablets present translations of
works dating from a much earlier period, and in some
cases from a totally different language. We are familiar
with analogous processes in the New Testament, for it is
generally believed that the Gospels frequently give us a
Greek reproduction of our Lord's Hebrew addresses. Other
documents may have been modernized in their form and
language when passing through the hands of the prophetic
compilers.

It is exceedingly difficult to tell how far there was any need *Or modern-*
of modernization of Hebrew between the days of Moses and *ization?*
the period of the Captivity. The language seems to have
been in a fairly stationary condition, though it had its
tribal peculiarities from the time of the Judges onwards;
and the presence of people speaking kindred tongues,
both in and out of Canaan, would tend to introduce many
provincialisms, and perhaps a few barbarisms. The chief

men of Hezekiah's age knew Syrian (*i.e.* Assyrian), but their own language was not much affected by it. After the long sojourn in Babylonia, however, the case was different. The people's language must have been much affected with Chaldean expressions, hence the late forms in the books of this period, and the Chaldee sections in Ezra and Daniel; hence also we are told that when the Scribes read out of the Pentateuch in the days of Ezra they had to "give the sense"; in other words, to paraphrase the old text in more modern Hebrew, or, as it is usually called, Chaldee. Many a Scribe thus became a walking Targum; he was a diglot, if not a polyglot, and translation into another dialect would become a habit to him, as it was in later days to St. Peter and St. Paul.

Putting aside any further discussion of the characteristics of peculiar ages or writers, we wish to point out some peculiarities to be noted in the writing of Hebrew historians as a class.

Introduc-
tions and
summaries.   2. The writers frequently opened or clenched what they had to say with a few words of *introduction* at the beginning or of *summary* at the end. Sometimes they adopt both methods. This may be seen specially in the legislative parts of the Pentateuch. Thus in Lev. 8. 5 Moses says to the congregation, "This is the thing which the Lord commanded to be done." He then describes the whole series of ceremonies connected with Aaron's investiture. Again, in Lev. 6. 9, Moses is told to command Aaron and his sons, saying, "This is the law [ritual] of the burnt-offering"; details then follow. In Lev. 7. 37 we have a summary of all the preceding chapters, "This is the law of the burnt-offering, of the meat-offering, and of the sin-offering, and of the trespass-offering, and of the consecra-tions, and of the sacrifice of the peace-offerings, which the Lord commanded Moses in Mount Sinai." The same method is adopted in some historical portions of the books.

3. There is an expression which frequently occurs in *" These are the genera-* Genesis—"These are the generations." There are two *tions."* quite distinct words translated "generation" in the Old Testament. The one (דור) seems to mark the course of time, as when we say, "from generation to generation." The other, *Toldoth* (תולדות), is in the plural number, and is used in a special sense. Literally, it signifies offspring or descendants, and is introduced in such prefatory sentences as Gen. **11**. 10, 27, "These are the generations of Shem," and "These are the generations of Terah." These two Hebrew words for generation are to be found together in Gen. **6**. 9. The word *Toldoth*, however, does not exactly stand for a genealogy; for this another word is used, and the two stand in juxtaposition in 1 Chron. **5**. 7 and **7**. 9. It rather marks *order of birth*, and hence gives a title to precedence and chieftainship, which is regarded as of high importance in Eastern life. This seems plainly the sense of the word in Exod. **28**. 10, where the stones of the breast-plate are ordered to be engraved with the names of the twelve sons of Jacob "according to their birth" (lit., after their generations). Compare Gen. **44**. 32. This sense may be illustrated by such passages as 1 Chron. **8**. 28, "These were heads of the fathers, by their generations, chiefs," *i.e.* they were chief men according to the order of their birth. See also 1 Chron. **26**. 31. In accordance with this view of the word we should interpret Gen. **25**. 12, 13, "Now these are the generations of Ishmael . . . and these are the names of the sons of Ishmael, by their names, according to their generations." See also Gen. **36**. 1, 9.

The expression "These are the generations" usually stands first and introduces certain names, as may be seen in the instances already cited, and in Ruth **4**. 18; but sometimes this or some similar expression may be found both at the beginning and the end of a list. Thus in 1 Chron. **1**. 29, 31, we read, "These are their genera-tions . . . These are the sons of Ishmael." So in Gen. **10**. 1, 32, "These are the generations of the sons of Noah . . .

These are the families of the sons of Noah after their generations"; and Exod. **6. 16, 19,** "These are the names of the
sons of Levi according to their generations . . . These are
the families of Levi according to their generations."

Sometimes this word goes further and signifies a family
history. In this sense we should probably interpret it in
Gen. **6. 9; 25. 19;** and **37. 2,** where we read, "These are the
generations [*i.e.* the family history] of Noah—of Isaac—of
Jacob" respectively.

Gen. 5. 1.   In Gen. **5. 1** we find the notable expression, "This is
the book of the generations of Adam. In the day that God
created man, in the likeness of God made He him; male
and female created He them; and blessed them and called
their name Adam, in the day when they were created."
The word here translated "book" (ספר) might be rendered
"list," but the Greek rendering is "book" (βίβλος), and
St. Matthew so gives it, with apparent reference to this
passage, at the beginning of his Gospel. The reference
from the passage before us to Gen. **1. 26–28** is very plain,
so that the verse looks both backwards and forwards—
backwards to the day of the creation of man, and forwards
to the order of descent from Adam onwards to Noah, and
to certain particulars of family history connected therewith.
In Num. **3. 1** we have a somewhat similar expression—"Now
these are the generations of Aaron and Moses in the day
that the Lord spake with Moses in Mount Sinai." A list
of the descendants of Aaron follows, but Moses' descendants
are not given; and it has been observed as a singular fact
that the descendants of Moses are passed over in the
Pentateuch, which would certainly not have been the case
if the book were a late production. His name, however, is
introduced into this verse because his family history had
already been given when God spoke with him at Horeb
(see Exod. **6. 16,** &c.). There is one other notable passage
where the expression occurs, viz., Gen. **2. 4:** "These are the
generations of the heavens and of the earth when they were
created, in the day that the Lord God made the earth and

the heavens." In this passage, as in the other two, we have
the words "in the day," and they seem to refer to the
previous piece of history, as in the other two cases. They
seem to point backwards and prepare the reader to go
forwards to a detailed account of some particulars included
under the general sketch already given. They bind into one
the "order of birth" of heaven and earth (chap. 1) the
"family history" of man (chaps. 2-4), and they may have
been introduced by Moses in his capacity of compiler.

4. Another peculiarity of Hebrew historic style is the *Fondness for repetitions.*
fondness for *repetitions*. This may be seen on a large scale
by comparing the two accounts of the Tabernacle, one being
the order for its construction, the other the report on its
completion, the latter going strictly through the details
given in the former (see Exod. 25-40). It may be seen
again in the seventh of Numbers, which contains no less
than eighty-nine verses, because the historian thought it
due to each tribe that all their offerings should be recorded,
though all the twelve princes offered identically the same.
It may be gathered also from the frequent repetition of
certain legislative enactments, ceremonial and social, *e.g.*
orders relating to the Passover, to blood, to the Sabbath,
to gleaning, and such-like.

This delight in repetition may be seen also in the structure
of the sentences. There was a semi-poetic tendency to
parallelism of thought and utterance in all old language,
and this clung to the descendants of Abraham through all
their literary history, down at least to the times of St. James
and St. John. This may account for such double sentences
as the following:—"And it came to pass . . . that two
of the sons of Jacob, Simeon and Levi . . . took each
man his sword and came upon the city boldly, and slew all
the males. . . . The sons of Jacob came upon the slain,
and spoiled the city . . . they took their sheep, and their
oxen, and their asses, and that which was in the city, and
that which was in the field, and all their wealth, and all

their little ones, and their wives took they captive, and
spoiled even all that was in the house" (Gen. **34.** 25–29).
"The children of Israel did eat manna forty years, until
they came to a land inhabited; they did eat manna until
they came unto the borders of the land of Canaan" (Exod.
16. 35). "The sons of Rimmon, Rechab, and Baanah, went,
and came about the heat of the day to the house of Ish-
bosheth, who lay on a bed at noon. And they came thither
into the midst of the house . . . and they smote him under
the fifth rib, and Rechab and Baanah his brother escaped.
And they went into the house, and he lay on his bed in
his bedchamber, and they smote him, and slew him, and
beheaded him," &c. (2 Sam. **4.** 5–7).

A style which seems to us cumbrous was natural to these
ancient recorders. They delighted in reiterating names and
in reaffirming events. Sometimes there was a special reason
for this reiteration. In Lev. **7.** 29 we read, "He that offereth
the sacrifice of his peace-offerings unto the Lord shall bring
his oblation to the Lord of the sacrifice of his peace-offerings."
This seems tautology to us, but the strong reaffirmation prepared the way for what was coming. Thus it is plain that
the tendency to reiterate in the same or in varied words was
innate in the Hebrew writer. It does not of itself show
double authorship or the blending of two narratives into
one.

Variations in use of proper names.   5. A fourth peculiarity has to do with *proper names.*
Various persons and places had more names than one, and
the writers sometimes varied them strangely. Thus in
Judg. **8.** 29 we read, "And Jerubbaal the son of Joash
went and dwelt in his own house," but the next verse proceeds, "And Gideon had threescore and ten sons," and the
32nd verse tells us that "Gideon the son of Joash died," &c.
Some names are used consistently throughout, *e.g.* Abram
and Abraham, but in the case of certain places the new
names are introduced into the narrative before they were
really given. In Gen. **12.** 8 Abraham is said to have pitched

his tent near Bethel, but Bethel was in those days called Luz. So in the case of Gilgal (Josh. **4.** 19; compare **5.** 9), Bochim (Judg. **2.** 1 and 5), Lehi (**15.** 9 and 17), Ebenezer (1 Sam. **4.** 1 and **7.** 12). It is only in the first of these cases any real difficulty arises, and the introduction of the word "Bethel" for "Luz" must be due to the hand of Moses and not to that of Abraham, from whose brief record or instruction the history of Gen. **12** must have been compiled.

6. Attention might also be called to Hebrew ways of reckoning days and years, which are so different from our own; also to the tendency to round numbers, as seen in the seventy souls which went down to Egypt, and the forty years' period of rest in the Book of Judges, and the three sets of fourteen generations in St. Matthew. *Ways of reckoning.*

7. We must not forget to point out that the Hebrew historian's method of arranging materials is not always like ours. This is notably the case in the Books of Kings, where the compiler had to carry on two concurrent streams of history, passing from one to the other as best he could. We cannot but marvel at the skill with which he accomplished this difficult task, condensing so much into a small compass without losing sight of pictorial details. Nor can we withhold our admiration from the Chronicler, who repeated so much that was already written, whilst adding some striking scenes from other sources, and who blends the whole so well that we should never know that we were reading a compilation had we not the Book of Kings before us. *Skill of writers.*

These may seem small matters, but they have sometimes proved stumbling-blocks to critics, who have not always made due allowance for the ancient way of putting things which is so characteristic in these books.

Two important points have to be added, not so much of a literary as of a theological character.

8. First, the way of putting things all the way through from Moses to Nehemiah is essentially *religious.* Even in *Theological style of the writers.*

the Book of Esther, where the name of God is not to be found in the Hebrew text, there is a profound sense of Providence which seems to be longing for an utterance, and to which the Septuagint has given free expression. Oriental writings and conversations, even where the subject is quite secular or trivial, are strongly tinged with theological expressions; but the Old Testament gives us something more than this. God is the chief actor throughout. All that is done upon earth, He doeth it. The Lord works salvation; the Lord hardens the heart; the Lord speaks the word; the Lord raises up generals, and brings rain, and sends locusts, and punishes the disobedient. Not only the writers but the actors recognize the Divine immanence all the way through, even though in many cases their deeds belie their professions.

Anthropomorphism.   These theological convictions frequently find their expression in strongly anthropomorphic language. How else could they be expressed? If the Most High had not condescended to speak in human language, to adopt human analogies, and to make known His will and His ways in terms borrowed from the human mind and body, we do not see how revelation could have been accomplished. At the same time, the writers call our attention to the Lord's deeds as much as to His words. The two claim to be studied together, and each throws light on the other; but of the two, deeds are most intelligible, for they are plain to the meanest understanding, and they need no translation.

Biblical idioms.   9. Every attentive reader of the Bible is familiar with the fact that it abounds in expressions, idioms, figures, and groups of words, which constantly recur. They are of various classes. Some may be called simply Hebrew idioms, such as might be found in any non-religious book written in the language in early ages—had such existed—*e.g.* to be old and well stricken in years, to draw a bow at a venture, to dwell under one's own vine and figtree, to your tents (*i.e.* prepare for war), sheep without a shepherd, former rain and latter rain, latter days, a double portion, to speak comfortably, to smite under the fifth rib. Some of these expressions have a more forcible appearance in Hebrew than in English (*e.g.* an hairy man, with one consent, &c.). Another class leads one into greater depths of thought connected with the history and the hopes of the people. These may be taken as instances :—A stranger and a sojourner, to set one's house in order, to sleep with one's fathers, to be gathered to one's people, to give up the ghost, to go the way of all the earth, to walk with a perfect heart, to prepare the heart. A third class takes us to the verge of morals, providence, and theology, which, in fact, they presuppose ; *e.g.* the cry went up to heaven, thy blood be on thy head, he shall die in his iniquity, he shall bear his iniquity, the sons of the prophets, " fear not " (an expression occurring more than eighty times), man of God, land flowing with milk and honey ; or they have a history, *e.g.* to trouble Israel (see 1 Kings **18.** 17), a remnant that escapeth, mercy and truth, gracious and merciful, to dwell in the land safely, the land which I sware to give to your fathers.

We now come to those to which we desire specially to call *Sacred idioms.* attention, which include or directly imply the name of the Lord. The following are the most notable instances :—To profane God's holy name, holiness to the Lord, the Lord be witness, as the Lord liveth, the Lord do so to me and more also, the Lord be with thee, to find grace in God's sight, the Lord establish His Word, the Lord thundered, the Lord hath visited His people, the Lord raised up judges, the Lord appeared, the glory of the Lord appeared, I will be their God, the angel of the Lord, ye shall know that I am the Lord, the hand of the Lord was with him, blessed of the Lord, inquire of the word of the Lord, the Lord wrought salvation, the battle is the Lord's, the anger of the Lord was kindled, the fear of the Lord fell, the Spirit of the Lord fell upon a man, to seek the Lord, to inquire of the Lord, the Lord's hand is not waxed short, none like Me, no God like Me, the Word of the Lord came to a man, thus saith the

Lord, the Lord spake unto Moses saying, to tempt the Lord, the earth is the Lord's, in the name of the Lord, the cause was from the Lord.

These and similar expressions deserve careful study : their history is worth tracing. Some are characteristic of particular writers ; most of them have their origin in the Pentateuch. They show how the Divine interventions connected with the Patriarchal history and the Exodus stamped themselves upon the thought and language of the people. History creates language. Expressions such as those cited tend to lose their force as the centuries roll on, and we find many of them used by semi-idolaters in the period of the Kings; but they sprang out of realities. What theology there is in the title twice given to God by Moses, "the God of the spirits of all flesh "; what reminiscences in Solomon's words concerning the Lord that He dwelt in thick darkness; what force in the title given to God by Elijah and Elisha, "the Lord before whom I stand "; what pathos in Jacob's formula, "the angel that redeemed me from all evil bless the lads "; or David's "as the Lord liveth who hath redeemed my soul out of all distress " (1 Kings 1. 29) ; and what good sense in the way in which Abraham's servant approaches God as "the God of my master Abraham."

Summary.   We may say of all such expressions that they are a linguistic and theological inheritance. They indicate deep convictions concerning the existence of the one living and true God, to Whom heaven and earth belong, Who orders all things according to His own pleasure, and carried out His purposes of good through the special instrumentality of the descendants of Abraham, Isaac, and Jacob. In a word, they are a linguistic protest against naturalism and in favour of supra-naturalism.

CHAPTER XIV.

HISTORICAL CHARACTER OF THE BOOKS.

1. The Old Testament is to a large extent professedly *Further* and confessedly historical; and we have shown reason *tests proposed:* for assuming that the materials from which it is compiled are of a first-class character, being in the main contemporary and authoritative. The books in question have this peculiarity in them, that they are not confined to a purely internal history of the Hebrew family and people in its religious and social aspect, but they touch on external matters all the way through. The things which are recorded "were not done in a corner." Moreover they cover a great deal of ground. There are in round numbers 2,000 years between the age of Noah and that of Nehemiah. These facts taken together help us to test the character of the writings, and to find out if they are what we assume them to be.

2. There are two simple tests to which such works as *Internal.* those which we are discussing might be subjected. First, we may study the internal history of the whole period, and ask ourselves if it is a consistent narrative throughout. We say "consistent" not "continuous." There is manifestly no attempt at a continuous history. We have sketches, Antediluvian, Patriarchal, and Israelite; that is all. The more unsystematic and fragmentary they are, the less likely does it become that they are the products of a late age, and the easier would it be for the critic to detect imposture. Moreover, if these sketches are really ancient they will give details, whilst if the materials from which they are composed were late, details would be avoided as dangerous if not impossible to invent.

It is generally acknowledged that there are no material inconsistencies in the narrative as a whole. What apparent inconsistencies have been pointed out are usually considered as proofs that the compilers had before them different documents which regarded things from slightly different points of view—as in the similar case of the Four Gospels; others might prove to be no inconsistencies at all if we knew more of the circumstances of the times, and if we examined the language more minutely. More need not be said at present on this point, as it is practically passed over by modern critics. It should be added, however, that the vivid details of the Patriarchal narrative are strong evidences of the antiquity of the documents from which they are composed.

External. 3. The second test is of great importance. It arises out of the fact that Biblical history presents so many points of contact with the doings of outside nations. We ask how far these references are borne out by external evidence.

It is instructive to note the change which the discoveries of the last half-century have produced on the discussion of this question. If we look back to the old standard book on "The Connection between Sacred and Profane History," by Prideaux and Shuckford, we find that Herodotus, Manetho, Josephus, and a few other writers supply the chief materials for comparison with the Sacred Histories. But it is not so now.

We may divide the references in the Hebrew books to external matters thus :—

i. There is the Antediluvian period, partly cosmic and partly Adamite, reaching to the Deluge.

ii. There is the Patriarchal age, covering the whole period between the Deluge and the death of Joseph.

iii. There is the Israelite period, reaching on to the time of Nehemiah.

What have we now got in the way of illustration of the Biblical narrative through these three periods?

For the first, we have the Chaldean " Genesis," *i.e.* the Creation Tablets, and the Deluge Tablets, with which we may perhaps associate the tablets relating to Babel.

For the second, we have the old Babylonian bricks and records on the one hand, and the papyri, *stelæ*, and other monuments of Egypt.

For the third, we have the later Egyptian remains, and the Assyrian, Neo-Babylonian, and Persian slabs, tablets, and cylinders.

These treasures are daily accumulating. We are becoming familiar with the Egyptian dolls, go-carts, and tops which Joseph's children may have played with. Older and yet older papyri are brought to light; depth beneath depth of literary treasure is brought forth from Mesopotamia. Meanwhile, Jerusalem itself has been riddled with shafts and tunnels at the hand of our explorers, and the surrounding regions are beginning to yield up their spoil. Dibon in the east, and Gezer in the west, and now Lachish also, speaking, as from the dust, concerning the days of the Judges and Kings.

4. The results are now in all men's hands. Thanks to *Results of discoveries.* such men as the Rawlinsons and Professor Schrader, and to the more popular writings of Sayce, Tomkins, and Budge, the secrets of antiquity are no longer veiled. Many things still remain unknown. We cannot, for example, yet decide who was the Pharaoh of the Exodus. But light of a trustworthy character is thrown on the Biblical history all the way through, and the conviction has become deep and widespread that we are not following cunningly-devised fables of a late date when trusting ourselves to Moses and his followers, but that we have records of real events from the hands of contemporary writers.

The noteworthy fact is that the evidence brought to light in the last half-century has all gone one way. Palestine exploration, the disinterring of Egyptian remains, and the opening out of the ruinous heaps of Assyria, Babylonia, and

Persia, have spoken with consentient voice. They utter their joint testimony to the historical character of the Hebrew writings.

Would this have been the case, however, if the materials from which these books were written had been late fabrications? Certainly not. The illustrations are often of that class called "undesigned coincidences," and are of too subtle a character to accommodate themselves to the theory of a late origin of the books. At any rate, possessing as we do such strong *primâ facie* grounds for holding the antiquity and trustworthiness of the books, we hail with thankfulness the strong confirmation which God has in His providence afforded us by the discovery and decipherment of these records of the past.

We now proceed to examine three special elements in the books which largely contribute to their historical character, viz., their chronology, their genealogies, and their topography.

CHAPTER XV.

CHRONOLOGICAL ELEMENT IN BIBLICAL HISTORY.

1. The history contained in the Old Testament covers a *Biblical chronology.* great deal of time. It reaches from the beginning of all things to the age of the Persian Empire. It does not, however, include annals, nor is there one fixed chronological scheme running through the books, as would have been the case if the work had been compiled throughout by one hand or in one age. It will be worth our while to illustrate this point in some detail.

2. The fifth of Genesis traces the human history from *Pre-patriarchal eras.* Adam to Noah; and whether we take the shorter period given in the Hebrew text, or the longer supplied by the Septuagint, still we feel that we possess the ancient traditional line of the Antediluvian fathers, with their ages; the year being, no doubt, the Babylonian one. The record of the Deluge is thoroughly chronological. We are told that on the seventeenth day of the second month in Noah's 600th year the Flood began, and we have enumerations of days and weeks till we get to the twenty-seventh day of the second month in the following year, when the earth was dry—the additional ten days turning the lunar year into a solar.

3. The twelfth of Genesis gives us the chronology of the *Patriarchal chronology.* Patriarchal line from Noah to Abram; and from that point and onward we get to personal narrative, and there is no further need of a chain of lives. There are plenty of indications, however, that the rest of the Patriarchs kept their reckoning carefully; in fact, we have a series of

undesigned chronological coincidences which may be briefly pointed out. Taking Abram's birth as, in round numbers, 2000 B.C., we find that he left Charran when he was 75; Isaac was born when Abraham was 100 (B.C. 1900); Jacob and Esau were born when he was 160; so that when he died, aged 175, his twin grandsons were 15 years old. A hundred years after the birth of Abraham Esau married Judith and Bashemath; 37 years later Jacob became a fugitive, being 77 years old. Isaac did not die for another 43 years, though we need not imagine him lying on his deathbed all these years, as a late critic grotesquely supposes. Still less need we magnify them into 80, as this critic does (*Contemp. Rev.*, Feb., 1890). Three hundred and sixty years (a year of years) after Abraham's birth Joseph died, say about 1640 B.C., and here the ancient family records come to an end. The chronology they contain is consistent throughout, though it is only introduced incidentally, and without any fixed era, such as the *annus mundi* which the Jews now adopt.

Era of the Exodus. 4. We now pass on to Exodus, and we gather from chap. **12**. 40 that a record of time had been kept since the Patriarchal age. The Hebrew text runs thus—"The sojourning of the children of Israel which they sojourned in Egypt was 430 years." The Samaritan Pentateuch and the LXX. add after the word Egypt "and in the land of Canaan"; this gloss seems intended to show that the sojourning was reckoned from some particular point in the Patriarchal history; and so Josephus (*Ant.* ii. 15. 2) says: "430 years after Abraham came into Canaan, but 215 only after Jacob removed into Egypt." It will be found on pursuing the details indicated in the chronological skeleton given above that between the time when Abram settled in Palestine (when he was 75) and the time when Jacob settled in Egypt there was a period of 215 years. It thus seems highly probable that the gloss is right, and that the writer of Exodus begins his chronology with the period of

Abram's becoming a sojourner in Canaan and Egypt (see Gen. **12**. 10). But what of Gen. **15**. 13, where we read of *Gen.* 15. 13. four centuries of affliction? The period here recorded probably starts from the time when the revelation was made. This at least is implied in the accentuation of the Hebrew, which introduces a pause (^) under the word "afflict-them" so as to separate it from the words "400 years," which are thus made to cover the whole verse. It is strange that the Revisers have not indicated this in their translation or punctuation of the passage.

The Exodus inaugurated a fixed era for Israel, and the Exodus-month began what we may call the ecclesiastical year (Exod. **12**. 2). The fourteenth day of that month initiated the Paschal Feast, which has been kept ever since at the same time. Various notes of time follow through the Pentateuch. Thus in Exod. **40**. 17 we are told that "in the first month in the second year, on the first day of the month, the Tabernacle was reared up." In Num. **9**. 1, "The Lord spake to Moses in the wilderness of Sinai in the first month of the second year, after they were come out of the land of Egypt, saying, Let the children of Israel keep the Passover at its appointed season." Num. **10**. 11, "On the twentieth day of the second month, in the second year, the cloud was taken up from off the Tabernacle of the testimony, and the children of Israel took their journeys." In Deut. **1**. 3 we have come to "the fortieth year, the eleventh month, and the first day of the month," the period of thirty-eight years having been spent in the region of Kadesh-barnea.

5. When Israel came into Canaan it would probably be *Chronology of the Judges.* the business of the priest to keep the calendar, but we do not find the Exodus era often referred to. There are, indeed, some important chronological coincidences and notes of time, *e.g.* in the words of Caleb (Josh. **14**. 7, 10), and in the speech of Jephthah (Judg. **11**. 26); but generally we have periods referred to in round numbers, *e.g.* in the well-known expression "the land had rest forty years." The

Books of Samuel chiefly comprise personal narratives. They have their chronology, as when we are told that the Ark was absent twenty years (1 Sam. **7.** 2); but the compilers of Joshua, Judges, and Samuel do not give us an exact system of dates starting from the Exodus.

1 *Kings* 6. 1.   When, however, we reach 1 Kings **6.** 1 we find an indication that the Exodus era had been retained all through. The verse runs thus: "And it came to pass in the 480th year after the children of Israel were come out of the land of Egypt, in the fourth year of Solomon's reign over Israel, in the month Zif (which is the second month), that he began to build the house of the Lord." The LXX. reads 440 instead of 480, possibly reckoning from the end of the forty years of wilderness-wandering instead of the beginning. It is the custom of some critics to regard this verse as spurious, but there is no MS. authority for such a course. The verse must be taken—liable to the variation of reading—as part of the book, and with the aid of the passage in Exod. **12.** 40, it incidentally supplies us with the materials for completing a system of Biblical chronology. It is clear that the numbers are not arrived at by putting together the figures as they appear at first glance in the earlier books, for this would imply at least another hundred years, as Josephus seems to have found out.

Regal period.   6. During the Regal period we hear no more of the Exodus era. Dates are arranged by the accession of the kings, and when the history of the two kingdoms is being recorded, the accession of a king in one country is set against the year of the king in the other. It is not very easy for us to keep count of the actual chronology, though the people themselves could do so through means of the priestly Feast Calendar, and we occasionally have references to long periods—notably in the case of the 390 year-days of Ezek. **4.** 5.

Babylonian and Persian eras.   In 2 Kings **25.** 8 we meet for the first time with a foreign chronological era, namely, the accession-year of Nebuchad-

nezzar; whilst the later books of Ezra, Esther, Nehemiah,
and also Haggai and Zechariah, date from the accession of
the Persian monarchs.

In subsequent ages we find the era of the Seleucidæ *Later Jew-*
(312 B.C.) adopted by Jewish writers; see, for example, *ish chrono-*
1 Mac. **1.** 10, where we read that Antiochus "reigned in the *logy.*
137th year of the kingdom of the Greeks." This era was
also used for monumental inscriptions. (For instances, see
Proceedings of the Biblical Archæological Society, June,
1886.) Another era was used for a short time, viz., the
Maccabean. Thus we read in 1 Mac. **13.** 42, "Then the
people of Israel began to write in their instruments and contracts 'in the first year of Simeon the high priest, the
governor and leader of the Jews.'" This was used for
coinage in that age (see 1 Mac. **15.** 6), but was of course
temporary. All these eras passed away, and the Jews
finally resorted to the *annus mundi*, which they still retain
as their era.

7. To what conclusion does this review of Biblical *Summary.*
chronology lead us? We find it to be a growth, and a
natural growth. Each stage is adapted to the surrounding
history; a bare outline for the earliest period, exact details
for the Diluvian era, family dates for the Patriarchal age,
Exodus dates for wilderness life, an outline for the Judicial
period, regal dates for the kings, and foreign dates for the
Captivity and post-Captivity period. This falls in with the
conviction already arrived at, viz., that the books are the
bonâ fide work of the periods to which they respectively
profess to belong.

8. A few words may be added on *the divisions of time* *Hebrew*
amongst the Hebrews. The Patriarchs brought their *divisions*
reckoning and division of time from Chaldæa, the original *of time.*
birthplace of astronomy and chronology. It is true that the
subdivision of the day into twelve or twenty-four hours is
not so much as hinted at in the Old Testament; but there

were certain periods, as day, night, morning, evening, yesterday, to-morrow; together with peculiar forms of expression for noon, dawn, "between the two evenings," twilight, " cool of the day," &c. They had their week of seven days as the Chaldæans had, the seventh day in each case being named Sabbath (Chald. *Sabattu*), *i.e.* Rest-day. They also had their month of thirty days, and their year of twelve months or 360 days, an intercalary month being introduced once in three years so as to bring the lunar and solar years into fair harmony.

The months. 9. The months are usually designated by their order, without being named. Thus we read of the second month in Gen. **7. 11**, and the tenth month in Gen. **8. 5.** The Hebrew word usually translated month means "new" (חֹדֶשׁ), and is sometimes rendered "new moon." The other and less frequent word (יֶרַח) is supposed by some to refer to the pale yellow colour of the moon.

The months, however, are occasionally named, and it is interesting to compare their names with those used by the Babylonians and Assyrians. They run thus :—

BABYLONIAN.	JEWISH.
1. Nisannu.	Nisan—the first (Esther **3. 7**).
2. Airu.	Zif—the second (1 Kings **6.** 1).
3. Sivanu.	Sivan—the third (Esther **8. 9**).
4. Duzu.	
5. Abu.	
6. Ululu.	Elul (Neh. **6. 15**).
7. Tasritu.	Ethanim—the seventh (1 Kings **8.** 2).
8. Arah-Samna.	Bul—the eighth (1 Kings **6.** 38).
9. Kislimu.	Chisleu (Neh. **1. 1**).
10. Tabitu.	Tebeth—the tenth (Esther **2.** 16).
11. Sabatu.	Sebat—the eleventh (Zech. **1. 7**).
12. Addaru.	Adar—the twelfth (Esther **3.** 13).

It will be seen on examining this list that all the months that agree in name with the Babylonian list are in post-

Captivity writings, whilst the months mentioned in the Book of Kings have non-Babylonian names. The inference is obvious, viz., that the Israelites had their own names for the months up to the period of the Captivity, and afterwards they took the calendar of their conquerors. To this must be added that the month Nisan was called Abib in the law of Moses (see Exod. **13**. 4). The word Abib means "green ears"; at least so it is rendered in Lev. **2**. 14, the only place where it occurs except as the name of a month. It is thought by some that the word is of Egyptian origin, and this seems highly probable.

Here again, then, we have an interesting evidence of what may be called the stratification of the books. If the writings which profess to be early were not really so, there would not have been these changes in the names of the months.

CHAPTER XVI.

THE PRIMITIVE GENEALOGIES OF ISRAEL.

Genealogies in the Old Testament. 1. Few subjects connected with Old Testament criticism are more interesting, and at the same time more perplexing, than the study of the genealogical system which pervades the books. Almost everyone who comes upon the scene is introduced as the son of someone else. We are all familiar with such groups as the following :—Bezaleel the son of Uri, Jeroboam the son of Nebat, Micaiah the son of Imlah, Jehonadab the son of Rechab, Zedekiah the son of Chenaanah, Elisha the son of Shaphat, Jehu the son of Jehoshaphat, the son of Nimshi, or (as it is usually put for brevity's sake) Jehu the son of Nimshi. The earlier and later books agree in this method of identifying persons by their fathers, giving, so to speak, a surname with a personal name.

Pedigrees. We are also familiar with the plan of introducing persons of considerable importance with a longer list of ancestors, who are frequently traced back to some very ancient Head. Thus Achan is designated (Josh. 7. 18) as the son of Carmi, the son of Zabdi, the son of Zerah, of the tribe of Judah. Elkanah is introduced (1 Sam. 1. 1) as the son of Jeroham, the son of Elihu, the son of Tohu, the son of Zuph, an Ephrathite. Kish is described (1 Sam. 9. 1) as the son of Abiel, the son of Zeror, the son of Bechorath, the son of Aphiah, a Benjamite. Ahiah the priest is called (1 Sam. 14. 3) the son of Ahitub (Ichabod's brother), the son of Phinehas, the son of Eli, the Lord's priest in Shiloh. When David is first mentioned in the First Book of Samuel (chaps. 16. 1 ; 17. 12), we are only told that he was one of the eight sons of Jesse the Ephrathite of Bethlehem-Judah ; but the Book of Ruth contains his genealogy in a form which reminds us of the genealogy of our Lord given by St. Matthew.

It runs thus :—"Now these are the generations of Pharez : Pharez begat Hezron, and Hezron begat Ram, and Ram begat Amminadab, and Amminadab begat Nahshon, and Nahshon begat Salmon, and Salmon begat Boaz, and Boaz begat Obed, and Obed begat Jesse, and Jesse begat David " (Ruth **4**. 18–22).

Ezra the scribe introduces himself (chap. **7**. 1–5) as the son of Seraiah, the son of Azariah, the son of Hilkiah, the son of Shallum, the son of Zadok, the son of Ahitub, the son of Amariah, the son of Azariah, the son of Meraioth, the son of Zerahiah, the son of Uzzi, the son of Bukki, the son of Abishua, the son of Phinehas, the son of Eleazar, the son of Aaron the chief priest. This is a grand genealogy; but probably not an exceptional one, though we possess few such pedigrees except in the Book of Chronicles. *Ezra's pedigree.*

Enough has now been advanced to illustrate the point with which we start, viz., that the Old Testament is pervaded with genealogies. The importance of these genealogies to their possessors was very great indeed. They were the title-deeds of each family, giving them a claim on the inheritance of their fathers (see 1 Kings **21**. 3). To us their interest is mainly historical. They are the backbone of the sacred history. By a careful study of them we get some ideas of the tribal and intertribal life of Israel. By comparing them with one another we also obtain confirmation of the chronological system of the Old Testament. Moreover, they have a bearing on the respective ages of the books which contain them.

It is to this last point to which we now desire specially to call attention. But before doing so it is necessary to mark some of the peculiarities of the Hebrew genealogical system as a whole.

2. These pedigrees seem to have been kept in two forms. Some started from the head of a tribe or family and traced down through a certain line, disregarding all accessory branches, and reaching a particular person. These are the *Forms of pedigrees.*

most formal. Our Lord's genealogy given in St. Matthew is the most familiar instance. Others began at the bottom, with the person who is to be spoken about, and traces his pedigree back to an early and well-known ancestor. Such is the genealogy of our Lord given by St. Luke. The former may be called family pedigrees, which would be constantly added to ; the latter are personal pedigrees, and are based on the former. It is a curious thing that in 1 Chron. 6 we have two pedigrees of Samuel's family : the first starts with Kohath the son of Levi, and reaches down to Samuel's sons (verses 22–28) ; the second starts with Heman the singer, the grandson of Samuel, and traces up to Kohath the son of Levi, the son of Israel. Any student who writes the two lists in parallel columns and compares them will be at once introduced to some of the puzzles of the Hebrew genealogist.

Omissions in pedigrees.   3. It seems to have been part of the Hebrew system to leave out subsidiary names in certain lines when not of importance, or not needed for the purpose of identification. Hence, as we have already pointed out, Jehu is called the son of Nimshi, though he was really his grandson ; Zechariah the prophet was called the son of Iddo by his contemporaries (see Ezra 6. 14), though he was really the son of Berechiah, the son of Iddo (Zech. 1. 1). The Hebrews had no word for grandfather or grandchild, and the words father, mother, son, daughter, frequently indicated the line of ancestry rather than the particular step in the line. Maachah, the daughter of Abishalom, is called the mother of Abijam (1 Kings 15. 2), and also the mother of Abijam's son Asa (1 Kings 15. 10), where we must understand—as in the margin—"grandmother." The Babylonian queen, or queen-mother, speaks to Belshazzar of his father Nebuchadnezzar (Dan. 5. 11), but Belshazzar was three, or perhaps four, steps removed from Nebuchadnezzar. In the list of Ezra's ancestry which we have given above there are two, if not three, omissions, as will be seen by comparing the pedigree as given more fully in 1 Chron. 6. 1–15.

A further point to be observed is that not only were names *Double* pronounced, and consequently spelt, differently by different *names.* writers—a matter which we must discuss further on—but also that the same person sometimes had two names, the second being either entirely different, and given owing to some family whim or personal peculiarity, or having a certain resemblance which is unrecognizable at first sight. It was the doing of a particular deed that turned Gideon into Jerubbaal; it was an oft-repeated Hebrew fancy that turned Jerubbaal into Jerubbesheth; but why should Samuel's ancestor, who had the name of Uriel (God is light) be also called Zephaniah (the Lord is darkness)?

4. Leaving, however, this topic for the present, we have *Other pecu-* to call attention to other peculiarities in the Hebrew pedi- *liarities.* grees. A man might have several wives at the same time. Then there would be several families, and the mother's name becomes a matter of importance. In David's case we have two lists of his sons, one set born at Hebron, and one set born at Jerusalem; in the first of these lists the names of the mothers are carefully given (compare 2 Sam. **3**. 2–5, and chap. **5**. 13–16). Occasionally we have long lists of the children of various wives and concubines, as in the case of the elder Caleb (1 Chron. **2**. 18, &c.). Again, the genealogist sometimes enumerates the sons. Thus, whilst in 1 Sam. **17**. 12 Jesse is said to have eight sons, in 1 Chron. **2**. 13–15 we find them named and enumerated as the first, the second, and so on, David being the seventh. Thus one of the sons had disappeared from the list, for reasons which we need not now discuss.

5. Some of the persons named in the pedigrees died child- *Zerubba-* less (*e.g.* Seled, 1 Chron. **2**. 30). This point may have been *grce.* mentioned for family reasons, or to indicate where adoption came in. The line from which Zerubbabel sprang is a very remarkable one in this connection. Josiah is said to have had four sons (1 Chron. **3**. 15), namely, Johanan, Jehoiakim,

Zedekiah, Shallum. But when he died the people of the land took his son Jehoahaz and made him king. This Jehoahaz will be seen by reference to Jer. **22. 11** to be the fourth of Josiah's sons, viz., Shallum. After a reign of three months his brother Jehoiakim is put in his place. He is succeeded by his own son Jehoiachin or Coniah, of whom Jeremiah says (**22. 30**), " Write ye this man childless," which he explains as meaning that " none of his seed shall prosper, sitting upon the throne of David and ruling any more in Judah." By whom was Coniah succeeded? By his uncle Zedekiah, the third of Josiah's sons, who became a king. The chronicler (2 Chron. **36. 10**) calls Zedekiah " brother " to his predecessor, but the writer of the Kings (2 Kings **24. 17**) uses the more accurate, but cumbrous, expression " father's brother."

How was Zerubbabel related to these last kings? Was he the son of Pedaiah (according to 1 Chron. **3. 19**); or the son of Shealtiel (Salathiel) (according to Ezra **3. 2**, and Matt. **1. 12**)? And whose son was Salathiel? Was he a literal or adopted son or grandson of Coniah (1 Chron. **3. 17**, and Matt. **1. 12**), or the son of Neri (Luke **3. 27**)? Adoption must evidently come in here. Salathiel was by blood probably son of Neri, of Nathan's line, but by adoption he stood as the son or lineal representative of the house of Solomon.

Genesis pre-supposed throughout.   6. We need not pursue this particular point, but what we wish to call attention to is the fact that the Hebrew genealogists had methods of their own, and that the writer of the Chronicles gives the documents as they stood, without any attempt to make all the lists dovetail into one another. The lists are monumental rather than methodical, and yet beneath all the network of names in the Old Testament we may detect not only a scheme but also a growth; and that growth is absolutely dependent on the Book of GENESIS for its existence. The whole genealogical system presupposes the Patriarchal history. Let us look into this matter more closely.

The story of the birth of Jacob's twelve sons is given *Jacob's sons.* piecemeal in Gen. **29, 30,** and **35,** being interwoven with contemporaneous narrative. There is no indication of the future of any of the sons, but the reason why each got his peculiar name is given—this reason not always being based on etymology, but often springing out of a play on words. We take these chapters to be the original contemporary record to which the nation in all future time would look for information on this important subject. In Gen. **35.** 22–26 we have the complete list of the sons, and the only children of the next generation referred to at that stage are connected with a narrative of shame (Gen. **38**). Joseph's children are introduced in their natural place (Gen. **41.** 50–52). In chap. **46** we have a list of those who entered Egypt. The list is a very simple one, but of great historical importance. It consists of Jacob's children and grandchildren, with a very few great-grandchildren, who are confined to two or at most three out of the twelve families.

7. We now pass on to the Book of Exodus. It opens *Pedigrees in the age of Moses.* with a summary, which includes a verbal reference to the list given in Gen. **46.** 26, 27. In the sixth chapter the list is more fully referred to, in order to show the genealogy of Aaron and Moses (who for genealogical purposes are put in this order; contrast Exod. **6.** 13 and 26). We now reach the interesting point that instead of having to do with individuals we have to do with *families.* The word so translated (מִשְׁפָּחָה) is used in Genesis of the families of mankind generally, but not of Jacob's family. Now, however, at the period of the Exodus the original sons of Jacob are regarded as heads of families, or, as we might call them, *clans,* and the word is used constantly for the same purpose all the way through the Historical Books to the end of the lists in 1 Chron. **7.**

These families were regarded as subdivisions of the Tribes; *Tribal subdivisions.* but whence did the word "tribe" take its origin? There are two words translated "tribe" in the Old Testament.

H 2

The one (מטה) means a rod or staff. It is used of Judah's staff (Gen. **38**. 18), and of Moses' rod (Exod. **4**. 2), and first appears as signifying a tribe in Exod. **31**. 2, 6. It is used down to 2 Chron. **5**. 2 in this sense (though very seldom in Samuel and Kings). The other word (שבט), which also means rod or staff, is first used in Gen. **49**. 10, the "*sceptre* shall not depart," and is appropriated as the designation of the twelve tribes in the 28th verse. From this point on-wards it is freely used through the Old Testament. We gather that the historical origin of the tribal life of the sons of Jacob is traceable to the time of his death, whilst the subdivision into families appears later, viz., at the period of the Exodus. The families, again, were naturally sub-divided into houses or households.

On examining the list given in Exod. **6**. 14–26, we observe, first, that it only gives the outline of the first three tribes of Israel, the purpose being to reach as far as the line of Moses and Aaron; and, secondly, that it adds a few particulars which could not be given when Gen. **46** was written, viz., the ages of Levi, Kohath, and Amram at their respective deaths. Also, whilst in Genesis we have only Levi's three sons—Gershon, Kohath, and Merari—in Exodus we have the two next generations, which include Amram and his family, down to his great-grandson Phinehas, who is the connecting link between the period of the Exodus and the days of the Judges.

Pedigrees in the Book of Numbers. 8. Passing on to the Book of NUMBERS, we have the actual state of things concerning the tribes and their families at the time of the Exodus. In the first chapter we find that the twelve tribes are an organized body, under a certain amount of military discipline, subdivided into families, according to the houses of the fathers, with regular pedigrees, and with heads to the tribes. These princes were eminent men, and their names are quite a study in theology. They are answerable for the numeration of the people in the first chapter, and for their organization

in the second chapter, and they bring their special offerings,
all alike, in the seventh chapter. Their names were not
forgotten in after times. Thus the prince of Judah is
Nahshon the son of Amminadab; and in the pedigree of
Judah's family in 1 Chron. **2.** 10 we read " Amminadab
begat Nahshon, the prince of the children of Judah " (*i.e.*
the prince referred to in the Book of Numbers).

Another thing to be noticed in these chapters is that for
the first time Joseph's sons figure among the tribes, the
Levites being accounted for separately. The same is the
case in chap. **13**, where the spies are enumerated.

We now pass over the period of Wandering, or desert-
life, and find ourselves at its close. In Num. **26** a second
census is taken, and here we have an enumeration of the
families of Israel. Let the list be carefully compared with
that in Gen. **46**. The individuals are now heads of clans.
They are the same as before, though there are some variations of spelling, and a few omissions through the extirpation
of families; but no new families are introduced. The people
are organically the same. There is one other list in the
book containing the names of the responsible persons appointed to divide out Canaan, in conjunction with Eleazar
and Joshua. Only one of the original princes of the Exodus
is found in this list forty years later, viz., Caleb the son of
Jephunneh.

CHAPTER XVII.

GENEALOGIES IN THE LATER BOOKS.

Genealogies in the Chronicles. 1. In the last chapter we traced the tribal genealogies down from their source in the Patriarchal age to the close of the Desert period. Our business now is to examine the later books, and inquire how the genealogies which they contain stand towards the earlier lists.

The Books of Chronicles are related to Samuel and Kings in very much the same way as Numbers and Deuteronomy are related to Exodus and Leviticus. The first part of the Chronicles is genealogical. It is put together on a peculiar plan; and however deeply we study it, the key to its system frequently slips from our hand.

There cannot be any doubt that the division of the land amongst the families of which each tribe was composed led to the careful keeping of family pedigrees, copies of which would be preserved in tribal or national archives, under the safe keeping of scribes, priests, or recorders. Headship was hereditary; but it had to be proved from time to time. Villages were colonies, and every colony had its hereditary prince or sheikh (see, for example, 1 Chron. 4. 33 and 38).

Revision of pedigrees in David's time. 2. From time to time there seems to have been a public revision of these lists of headmen, and an examination of the pedigrees. Notably this was the case in the time of David, and probably the period in which he took the census was a very busy one. There was an "account of the chronicles of king David" (1 Chron. 27. 24), in which such things were recorded. In fact, he was as systematic as a Roman emperor in his method of administration, and it is one of the objects of the Book of Chronicles to set this forth. Thus we have in 1 Chron. 11 a list of his mighty men, which should be read alongside of the list in 2 Sam. 23. In chap. 12 we have the names of his early helpers, "men of war, who could keep rank, and who came to him with a perfect heart" out of every tribe. This is a remarkable list, bearing the marks of being contemporary, and secured for all time through its being incorporated in the Book of Chronicles. Then we come to the divisions of the descendants of Aaron into twenty-four courses, concerning which we read that "Shemaiah the son of Nathanael the scribe, one of the Levites, wrote them before the king" (1 Chron. 24. 6).

In the following chapter we have the families of Asaph, Heman, and Jeduthun, the heads of the musical and choral body; in chap. 26 we have the subdivisions of the porters or gatekeepers, and also of the treasurers, who were descendants of Moses, and who had charge of all the dedicated things. Military and civil headships are enumerated in chap. 27. A twelve-fold or tribal division is to be seen in most of David's arrangements, whilst in others we see his wisdom in securing experienced men for taking charge of civil departments (see, e.g., 1 Chron. 27. 25–31).

Now, all these arrangements were not the work of a moment. As we read these chapters we feel two things—one is, that we are studying contemporary documents; the other is, that the civil, political, and religious constitutions which David stamped upon Israel, and which tended, humanly speaking, to weld them into a model kingdom, were a growth, and sprang out of certain pre-existing elements which he found ready to his hand, and for which the previous history, legislation, and tribal arrangements of the people prepared the way.

3. We know not what genealogical works were prepared by Iddo the seer (see 2 Chron. 12. 15), but we pass on to another great period of revising the genealogies, viz., the days of Jotham and Hezekiah. In 1 Chron. 5. 17 we read: "All these were reckoned by genealogies in the days of

Pedigrees in the days of Jotham and Hezekiah.

Jotham king of Judah, and in the days of Jeroboam king of Israel." Who are the persons referred to as "all these"? They appear to be certain Gadites dwelling in Bashan. There is a Reubenite list somewhat later, *i.e.* in the time of the Captivity by Tiglath-pileser (chap. **5.** 4). The list in the half-tribe of Manasseh is of this period also (chap. **5.** 23–26). These lists are sadly brief, and when we compare them with the original descendants of Jacob, we find it almost impossible to trace the connection.

The family of Simeon is much less obscure. Their villages are given as in the time of David, and their princes as in the time of Hezekiah (chap. **4.** 31 and 41). The seventh chapter gives us the line of Issachar, Benjamin, Naphtali, Manasseh (the western half), Ephraim, and Asher. In all these cases the families are linked on to the old line of Jacob, and the numbers given appear to be the fighting men of the time of David. The eighth chapter seems to be added so that the names of the Benjamite inhabitants of Jerusalem might be preserved. It is to be noticed that this list includes the descendants of Meribaal (Mephibosheth), the son of Jonathan, for several generations, which would take probably to the period of the Captivity.

The genealogies were kept up to that time with some degree of accuracy, and were apparently attached to the book of the kings of Israel and Judah (1 Chron. **9.** 1), which we take to be the original and comprehensive work from which our Books of Kings were condensed, and from which large portions of the Chronicles were extracted.

The latest of the Biblical pedigrees.   4. Some of the lists in the book extend through a very long period. Whilst the first two chapters take us from the beginning of all things to the period of David, the third carries on his line to the grandchildren of Zerubbabel, and possibly much further. This depends upon the date of Rephaiah (verse 21). If the Shemaiah son of Shecaniah mentioned in this verse is "the keeper of the east gate" (Neh. **3.** 29), then the chronicler takes us three generations after the time of Nehemiah. It will be observed that David's representative in the days of Ezra is Hattush (Ezra **8. 2**). Possibly he is the Hattush of 1 Chron. **3. 22**. The family of Aaron is also traced down to the time of the Captivity (chap. **6. 15**).

5. We have now only one more list in the Chronicles which we need comment on, viz., that contained in the ninth chapter. The second verse, which seems properly to begin the chapter, runs thus: "Now the first inhabitants that dwelt in their possessions in their cities were Israel, the priests, the Levites, and the Nethinim. And in Jerusalem dwelt of the children of Judah, and of the children of Benjamin, and of the children of Ephraim and Manasseh." On turning to the opening verses of Neh. **11** we read (verses 3 and 4): "In the cities of Judah dwelt every one in his possession in their cities, Israel, the priests, the Levites, and the Nethinim, and the children of Solomon's servants. And at Jerusalem dwelt of the children of Judah, and of the children of Benjamin." The resemblance between the passages is striking, and the omission of the reference to Ephraim and Manasseh in the latter passage equally so. If the Chronicler is giving an account of the inhabitants of Jerusalem in the age of Nehemiah it is curious that he should introduce, or that the other account should omit, the descendants of Joseph.

1 Chron. 9 in relation to Neh. 2.

When we proceed to compare the chapters minutely we find that we have either the same persons or at any rate the same lines. First we have the descendants of Pharez, the son of Judah, David's ancestor, represented by Uthai in one list, and by Athaiah (which is practically the same name) in the other. Next come the Shilonites (*i.e.* the descendants of Shelah, see Num. **26. 20**), represented in each list by Asaiah (or Maaseiah). Then the sons of Zerah, whom the chronicler reckons at 690, but whom the writer of Neh. **11** omits (see, however, verse 24, where one of the line is mentioned).

The sons of Benjamin follow in both accounts, the names being nearly related, but not altogether parallel.

Then come in each account lists of priests, of Levites, and of porters (*i.e.* the hereditary gatekeepers of the Temple). After this the lists seem to drift apart, the chronicler going off into the specific duties of the Levites, and Nehemiah's list going into further particulars concerning the dwelling-places of the people in his time.

Anyone who will take the trouble to write out the lists contained in these chapters in parallel lines will appreciate the perplexities which they cause to the critical genealogist. On the one hand there is such an intimate relationship, on the other there are such bewildering variations. It is not our present business to deal with these difficulties, but rather to point out that there was a vital continuity between the dwellers in Jerusalem before and after the Captivity. The old Davidic arrangements were kept up as far as possible, the old families renewed their hereditary offices, and the lines of Judah, Benjamin, and Levi retained their position, carrying on the traditions and preserving some of the sacred deposits which had travelled down from past ages. Thus there is a "succession" all the way down through the ages from the Patriarchs to the Restoration—a period of about sixteen centuries. Is not this succession unique? Can we over-estimate its historical value?

Other pedigrees in Ezra and Nehemiah.   6. We must not, however, omit to notice certain other lists in the Books of Ezra and Nehemiah.

When Jeshua and Zerubbabel led back the first company of people into their old land they recorded the names of the heads of the families (see Ezra 2). They begin, as other lists did, with Parosh (? Pharez); then follow a number of headmen representing the city and village families who had been deported by Nebuchadnezzar. Then come the priests, the Levites, the porters, the Nethinims, and the children of Solomon's servants; the Nethinims being probably Gibeonites (see Ezra 8. 20), and the servants

of Solomon being the descendants of the original Canaanites
(see 1 Kings **9.** 21).

Ezra also gives us the names of those who accompanied
him on his return (chap. **8**). Almost all the family names
are to be found in Zerubbabel's list just referred to.

A third list is given us at the end of the book, enumerating
the names of those who had taken strange wives; and on
examining the names we find the same family lines for the
third time.

Nehemiah gives us in his 10th chapter a list of the princes
and heads, with the priests and Levites. Here again we
have to a very large extent the same family names. We
are thus able to form a fair idea of the true Jerusalemite
families of that time.

If we try to get later down in history the materials fail *Neh.* 12.
us. The first half of the 12th of Nehemiah contains the
latest names in Old Testament history (except, perhaps,
those referred to in 1 Chron. **3.** 23, &c., which we have
already pointed out). We are told (verse 11), that Joiada
begat Jonathan and Jonathan begat Jaddua, but this verse
does not take us much further down in time (if at all) than
chap. **13.** 28, where Nehemiah says that he chased away
one of Joiada's sons. In the 22nd and 23rd verses we are
told that the list of the priests was kept to the reign of
Darius the Persian (*i.e.* probably Darius Nothus, B.C. 424),
and a list of the chief Levites was kept "in the book of
the Chronicles" up to the time of Eliashib's son, who was
Nehemiah's contemporary.

7. These facts, which can easily be verified, lead to a very *Summary.*
definite conclusion. The books which we have been studying cannot well have been compiled later than the time of
Nehemiah. There may have been a few notes of later date,
but to bring down the book to B.C. 300, as some propose, is
uncritical and irrational. So far our researches justify the
old tradition—that while Moses began the Canon, Nehemiah
practically closed it.

CHAPTER XVIII.

TOPOGRAPHICAL ELEMENT IN EARLY BIBLICAL HISTORY.

Topograph-
ical details
in the Old
Testament.
1. Considering the limited proportions of the books which we are discussing, and the small extent of the land of Canaan, the number of places named in the Old Testament is truly surprising. We may take it as a characteristic of the Hebrew writers that they are detailed and graphic in their topography. Not that they attempt anything in the way of formal description—the topography is strictly subordinate to the history; but it is sufficiently full and clear to supply a realistic groundwork for the events recorded; and, above all, it is accurate. Whatever opinion critics hold about the dates and authorship of the books, there is a general acknowledgment that the writers knew their own country well. Its hills and valleys, streams and fountains, wells and cisterns, cliffs and shoulders, eminences and watch-towers, standing stones and conspicuous trees—all these were familiar to the writers, and play their part in the story. Our belief in the fidelity of a writer would be rudely shaken if we found his topography to be at variance with the facts; but how is it with the Historical Books of the Old Testament? The microscope of criticism and of exploration has been brought to bear on their pages, and it would be a poor tribute to say they have come forth from the investigation without a flaw having been discovered; let us say, rather, that the critic has received an increasing conviction of their absolute fidelity. The Bible is still regarded as the most trustworthy handbook to Palestine.

Wealth of
Hebrew
language.
2. We must here call attention to a fact well known to Hebrew students, viz., that the Hebrew language is very rich in topographical expressions. A few illustrations of

this point may be given. The ordinary name for a city (*Ir*)
is used hundreds of times in the Old Testament. Another
word (*Kiriah*) is rarer, occurring only four times in prose
and about thirty times in the Poetic and semi-Poetic Books.
But in the Chaldee letters contained in Ezra **4** it occurs no
less than eight times. The cities in each case were very
small, as may be gathered from the fact that there were
124 of them in Judah. A third word is used to mark the
fortified or fenced cities. Villages were designated by four
distinct words. There was the "daughter," *e.g.* Num.
21. 25, to signify that they were offshoots from mother-
cities; there was the "compound" (חָצֵר), a word as old
as Gen. **25. 16**, and applicable to any temporary collection of dwellings; there was the "shelter" (*Kaphar*), or,
as the modern Arabs call it, *Kefr*, familiar to us as the
first part of the name Capernaum; and there was the
"hamlet," or "unwalled village" (פֶּרֶז), from which some
think the Perizzites got their name. The word translated
"suburbs" (except in 2 Kings **23. 11**) is supposed to
indicate pasture-land (מִגְרָשׁ), and is used of the Levitical
possessions in the Pentateuch, Joshua, the Chronicles, and
Ezekiel. The term used for the refuge cities is quite a
peculiar one (מִקְלָט), and is used consistently for this purpose in the Pentateuch, Joshua, and the Chronicles.

Many Hebrew names of places are descriptive if not *Descriptive*
pictorial, and this accounts for two or more places having *names.*
the same name. Thus, there are various Ramahs, Gebas,
Gibeahs, Mizpehs; also two Carmels, Bethlehems, Ophrahs,
Ephraims, Abels, and Morehs. For the same reason some
places have in the Hebrew a definite article before them, as
Sharon, Jeshimon, and Millo. There are also peculiar words
for special districts. Thus we read of the Region (lit.,
"cord," חֶבֶל) of Argob, the Plain (lit., "circle," כִּכָּר) of
the valley of Jericho. So we meet with the *Shephelah*,
or lowlands, between the hill country and the shore of
the Mediterranean, and the *Negeb* in Southern Judah, and

the *'Arabah*, or Jordan valley. The "plains of Mamre" (Gen. **18.** 1) are supposed to be oak-woods, Mamre itself being never named after the Book of Genesis.

Special words. There are other topographical distinctions in Hebrew which often escape our notice in English. All such distinctions come naturally to the writer who is living at the time and in the place concerning which he is writing; but they would be pitfalls to a later inventor. Their number is legion. Thus the ordinary word for the bank of a river is "lip" (שָׂפָה), but when Jordan overflows its banks a different word is used (נָדָה, Josh. **3.** 15; **4.** 18; 1 Chron. **12.** 15); a well is *Beer*, *e.g.* in Gen. **21.** 30; but in 2 Sam. **23.** 15, David is said to long for water, not out of a well (as the E.A.V. and R.V.), but out of a cistern or pit, with which he was familiar, at the gate of Bethlehem; whilst in Exod. **15.** 27, the twelve wells are properly twelve springs.

The ordinary word for a tree (עֵץ) is used in Gen. **18.** 4, 8, where Abraham is described as showing hospitality to the angels; but the tree in Ramah under which Saul abode (1 Sam. **22.** 6) is one of a special kind, perhaps a tamarisk (אֶשֶׁל). The same is the case with the tree of Jabesh-gilead, where the remains of Saul's family were deposited (1 Sam. **31.** 13). The oak which was by Shechem, mentioned in Gen. **35.** 4, and referred to again, though with slightly different pronunciation, in Josh. **24.** 26, is *Elah* (אֵלָה); but the oak under which Deborah, Rebekah's nurse, was buried (Gen. **35.** 8) is *Allon* (אַלּוֹן).

Monuments. 3. Trees sometimes became monumental, owing to their age and history, as in the case just mentioned; and the same must be said of certain stones and pillars, which were both memorials and centres of worship from the Patriarchal age onwards. All are familiar with Jacob's stone (Gen. **28.** 18), which he set up as a pillar, and which he revisited after many years (Gen. **35.** 14). On the latter occasion he poured a drink-offering and oil on it—an incident which shows that

it was what is now called a cup-stone, with a hollow at the
top. The stone of Bohan (Josh. **15.** 6 and **18.** 17), which
was a boundary mark between Judah and Benjamin, is supposed to be named from its standing out in the form of a
thumb (בֹּהַן). It is a natural eminence, and has been detected by M. Ganneau in the *hadjar el asbah* (*i.e.* finger-
stone). In Judg. **9.** 6 we are told that all the men of
Shechem gathered together and went and made Abimelech
king by the plain of the pillar that was in Shechem. Why
is this place so carefully specified? Because it was historic;
in fact, it was a sacred place. We read in Josh. **24.** 26 that
" Joshua wrote these words in the book of the law of God,
and took a great stone, and set it up there under an oak, that
was by the sanctuary of Jehovah. And Joshua said unto all
the people, Behold, this stone shall be a witness unto us; for
it hath heard all the words of Jehovah which He spake unto
us." This passage is important for many reasons. It is not
only the key to the verse in Judges cited above, but also (as
we have seen already) takes us back to the Patriarchal age
when the Shechem oak first appears (see Gen. **35.** 4).

There are other stones, notably Eben-ezer (the stone of *Sepulchres.*
help), which stood as memorials for future ages. The same
is the case with sepulchres; those who " slept with their
fathers" were naturally " buried with their fathers," and this
was the system from the time of the Patriarchs onwards;
though in the case of some of the kings this method was
deliberately departed from. The story of the purchase of the
burial-place of Abraham is told with great detail in Gen. **23**,
and referred to in later sections of the book (see Gen. **49.**
29–32). The tomb of Rachel, whose sad death is recorded
in Gen. **35.** 20, is referred to again in 1 Sam. **10.** 2. Neither
of these were forgotten in later days, and the sepulchre of
David was equally honoured and preserved (see Acts **2.** 29).

4. We have pointed out in a previous chapter that there *Stages in*
were certain stages of chronology answering to the supposed *topography.*
ages of the books; and the notes given above suggest that

something in the way of confirmation of our view may be gathered from a study of Biblical topography. Let us pursue this topic a little further. The Historical Books are based on three sets of materials, viz., the work of the Patriarchs, the writings of the Exodus period, and those of the age which begins with the settlement of Israel in the land of Canaan. We will examine them in this order.

Garden of Eden. The description of the position of Eden (Gen. 2. 8–14) is evidently a very ancient piece of geography. Some years ago Sir H. Rawlinson read a paper on "The Site of the Terrestrial Paradise," in which he discussed the passage. He suggested that *Gan-eden* (Garden of Eden) answered to the old Babylonian *Gan-duniya*, and that the four rivers of Eden answer to the four which are associated with Babylonia in the oldest inscriptions. If this is the case we must go a step further, for the Eden of the Bible is very high, having watershed in four directions; and we are led to the conclusion that the Babylonians had travelled down from a mountainous region to the comparative level in which they lived in later ages. The younger Delitzsch has entered at length into the geography of the passage before us in his treatise called "*Wo lag das Paradies*," and Schrader has followed in his steps. Our present business is simply to call attention to the antiquity of the description as we have it.

Ararat. The next geographical reference is to "the mountains of Ararat" (not Mount Ararat), where the ark rested (Gen. 8. 4). They were probably in the south-western region of Armenia, from which the stream of population would subsequently tend towards Mesopotamia.

Gen. 10. 5. The 10th of Genesis is regarded by all critics as of high importance. Kalisch justly says with regard to it that "this list is without a parallel in the whole range of ancient literature," and adds that it "forms an organic part of the composition of Genesis, being a direct continuation of the preceding section, and alluding to the Deluge which had just (?) taken place." Whilst referring to Prof. Rawlinson's

Origin of the Nations (Religious Tract Society) for an elementary treatment of the contents of the chapter, it is sufficient here to say that it does not profess to be a gazetteer of the world, but gives an outline of the relationship which existed between certain heads of families and tribes, partly ethnological, partly commercial, and partly geographical, from a Chaldean or Babylonian point of view. Its date may partly be fixed by the 19th verse, where the borders of Canaan are given as from Sidon to Gerar and Gaza, and so round by Sodom, Gomorrah, Adonah, and Zeboim, to Lasha. This must be a description given before the destruction of the cities of the plain, and of course before the change of the name Lasha (Laish) into Dan; and we may regard Abraham as the authority for it as it stands. In Schrader's note on this chapter, he points out that there is extant an ancient Babylonian geographical list (IV. Rawl. 38, No. 1), containing a record of sixty-eight towns and districts, and that it may be compared for general structure with the Biblical list; but the Biblical list is of a far more comprehensive character, and contains notes of great importance, *e.g.* the account of the building of Nineveh, and the proverbial expression concerning Nimrod, "the mighty hunter before Jehovah."

6. Attention might be directed to the names Babel, Ur, *Ancient names of places.* and Charran; also to Ellasar (Larsa) and Gutium (where our text reads Goim, or "nations," Gen. **14.** 1); but we must advance with the Patriarchs into Canaan. The records before us give the origin of many names, *e.g.* Bethel, Mahanaim, Zoar, Beer-sheba, Penuel, Succoth, Beer-lahai-roi; and notes supply the later name for some places, *e.g.* Ephrath (that is to say, Bethlehem), Gen. **35.** 19. If anyone will be at the pains to examine the whole evidence in Genesis, he will find that all is consistent with the view that the book is older than the time when Israel re-entered Canaan, a few notes only being of a later date; and that its contents are not consistent with the theory—if, indeed, there be any that hold it—that the book was an invention of a later period.

I

CHAPTER XIX.

THE TOPOGRAPHY OF THE LATER BOOKS.

Topography in Exodus. 1. When we reach the Book of Exodus we find ourselves breathing another air. We are no longer in the far East or in Canaan, but in the Delta and its neighbourhood. There is a river, but its name is not given—though a special Hebrew word is used for it; and there is a sea—not, indeed, described geographically, but named after something which grows in it. Very few Egyptian places are named, but special local details are furnished in connection with the crossing of the Red Sea. The outlines of the Sinaitic Wanderings can be followed by the present-day traveller, provided he can escape out of the hands of the modern Amalekites. We would refer to Major Palmer's work on *Sinai* (S.P.C.K.), and to Mr. Hull's papers, and to the proceedings of the Egyptian Exploration Society, for full particulars on the accuracy of this part of the Mosaic narrative.

We find ourselves at the end of the Pentateuch in the territory of Moab, the exact position being given in Deut. **1. 1.** It may be mentioned here that the nationalities of Canaan whom the Israelites were to dispossess are enumerated over and over again in Genesis, Deuteronomy, and elsewhere; not always in the same order, and with some slight variations. And it is noteworthy that the oldest list (Gen. **10.** 15, &c.) contains some names which subsequently disappeared from view.

Boundaries of Canaan. 2. The boundaries of the Promised Land are sketched very shortly in Gen. **15.** 18 as from the River of Egypt (El-arish) to the Euphrates. In Exod. **23.** 31 they are described as destined to extend from the Red Sea (*i.e.* its eastern fork) to the Sea of the Philistines (the Mediterranean), and from the desert (in the south) to the river, *i.e.* the Euphrates. Of these regions Israel must have had

a very vague idea, and in Deut. **2.** 24 they are expressed
somewhat differently. But the great passage is Num. **34.**
2–12. Here Moses gives the people a fairly complete outline, which they were to fill in, beginning at the south-east
with the Salt Sea and coming out at the River of Egypt
(El-arish), then up the western border till they could descry
Mount Hor (apparently Hermon), and so across to Hazar-
enan, and down by the Sea of Chinneroth to the Salt Sea.
Compare throughout the border-lines presented in vision to
Ezekiel (chap. **47.** 15–21).

3. There has been some discussion as to the names for the *Points of compass.*
points of the compass amongst the Hebrews. Some useful
notes on the subject will be found in the *Proceedings* of
the Biblical Archæological Society, February 6th, 1883. It
would appear from this paper that the Egyptians had the
true points, which were named :—N., *mer-t-meh* ; S., *mer-
t-res* ; E., *Bech* ; W., *am-urt*. The Assyrian N. was
really N.W., and the other points were located accordingly,
their names being :— N., *iltanu* ; S., *sutu* ; E., *sadu* ;
W., *acharru*. In each case, however, it is supposed that a
region rather than a point is indicated. It also appears that
in Assyria the person is sometimes supposed to be going
west, the east is at his back, north at his right, and south
at his left. How was it with the Israelite? He appears
to have looked towards the east, for which he had two
words, the sun-rising (מזרח), and that which is " before "
one (קדם). The west is the sun-set (מבוא), the evening
(מערב), the sea (ים). The north is the dark (צפון). The
south is represented by six words, of which the chief signify
the Wilderness, and *the right hand* (*Teman*). None of the
words are those adopted in Assyria or in Egypt. They look
Patriarchal. Perhaps further light will yet be thrown on
the subject through Accadian research.

4. The Book of Joshua has all the geographical marks of *Topography in Joshua.*
contemporary writing. See, for example, the local details
connected with the crossing of the Jordan (Josh. **1.** 14–16);

the origin of the name Gilgal (**5. 9**) ; the local description of
Ai, which was subsequently destroyed (**7. 2**) ; the origin of
the designation of the valley of Achor (**7. 26**; see Isa.
65. 10; Hos. **2. 15**) ; the positions of the northern kings,
some of whom are never heard of again (**11. 1–5**), and the
list of the Canaanitish kings and their territories (chap. **12**).
We are thus introduced to the partition of the land among
the tribes, contained in chapters **13 to 21**, which have
afforded so much guidance to the explorer. It will be
enough here to refer for particulars to Conder's *Tent-work
in Palestine*, and to the other works of the Palestine
Exploration Fund. It should be added that old names are
still found in Joshua, such as Geshuri, Jebusi, Baalah, and
Luz; and that the town-names of that age can be illustrated
from Egyptian sources, such as the record of the victories of
Tothmes III. and the adventures of the Egyptian Mohar.

In the later books.   5. The Historical Books that follow proceed in the main
on the lines laid down in Joshua, and are highly pictorial.
See, for example, Judg. **7. 1**; **9. 37**; **20. 31**; **21. 19**;
1 Sam. **14. 4**; 2 Sam. **2. 24**. We must refer for full
details as to the topographical accuracy of these books to
Mr. Harper's *Bible and Modern Discoveries*. We here
find valuable confirmatory evidence of the position which
we had reached by independent investigations, viz., that
· the books bear the marks of being compiled from trustworthy materials. They are not myth, but history.

Topography of Jerusalem.   6. Another method by which we may test the ages of the
books is to take one city or locality and trace its history
through the narrative. Let us do this with JERUSALEM.
This city is not actually named until we reach Joshua, but
we find indications of its existence much earlier. In
Gen. **14** Melchizedek, king of Salem, suddenly comes on
the scene and brings forth bread and wine. The locality
is marked " as the valley of Shaveh, *i.e.* the King's dale."
The word translated by the two terms, " valley " and
" dale," is *'Emek*, which signifies an open valley rather

than a gorge; and the same word is used in 2 Sam. **18. 18,**
where the King's dale is again referred to. There cannot
be a doubt that the note in Gen. **14. 17** identifies the place
with that in which Absalom's pillar was set up, and which
must probably have been near Jerusalem. There were two
'Emeks in this neighbourhood, viz., the valley of Rephaim
or the Giants (mentioned in the Historical Books), and the
valley of Jehoshaphat, only named in the Book of Joel
(3. 2, 12). The first of these is usually placed west of
the city, and the other east; and this last would be in all
probability the King's dale. Jerusalem is called Salem in
Ps. **76. 2,** and thus tradition and the circumstances of
the case seem to fix Melchizedek's city as in this locality,
although there have been writers of eminence who have
been attracted to another site near Shechem.

In Gen. **22** Abraham is ordered to the land of Moriah, to
a specific spot on a mountain, where he is to present his son
as an offering to God. We read of the mountain of Moriah
again in 2 Chron. **3. 1** as the site of the Temple; and in
each case the Hebrew word has a definite article before it,
showing that the name had a special meaning. What is this
meaning? Not high-land or table-land, as the Septuagint;
nor the "land of worship" according to the old Jewish
paraphrase; but the land of Vision, or rather Provision.
In each case there was a special vision or provision of God
for a particular purpose; and the old proverb of Gen. **22. 14**
("in the mountain of Jehovah there shall be provision") is
a connecting link between the two incidents. Here, as in
the case of Salem, there has been a tendency to move the
Abrahamic Moriah to the plains of Moreh, but on very
slender grounds (see Smith's *Bib. Dict., s. v.* Moriah).

In Gen. **10. 16** we find the Jebusite among the descend-
ants of Canaan, in company with the Hittite and the
Amorite; and in Num. **13. 29** and Josh. **11. 3** this clan is
described as inhabiting part of the mountain or hill-country.
Jebus is plainly identified with Jerusalem in a note in
Josh. **15. 8,** though the latter name is introduced instead of

the earlier in Josh. **10**. 1, &c. Thus we have apparently four names for one locality, viz., Salem, Moriah, Jebus, Jerusalem ; the last of the four having possibly grown out of the roots of the first two, and perhaps signifying Provision of Peace (see Ps. **122**. 6). Whether this be so or not, the point specially to be noticed is, that if the Pentateuch and Joshua had been late productions, we should not have had any of the existing perplexities and diversities of opinion as to these names.

After David's time all becomes clearer. The Jebusite fortress is taken and becomes the stronghold of Zion, and is called David's city, its inhabitants being absorbed in the larger Benjamite and Judean population which had grown up on the neighbouring eminences (see 1 Sam. **17**. 54). It thus becomes the Royal city and the centre of worship, and with its history the fate of Israel has been bound up ever since.

The Books of Kings and Chronicles tell us much concerning the architectural work and fortifications with which the city was beautified and strengthened by various kings ; and the Book of Nehemiah supplies full topographical details concerning the walls.

Summary.   7. On surveying the Biblical story of Jerusalem, we cannot fail to be struck with the incidental way in which the city grows upon us. Would it be so if the early books were late inventions ? Another point is noteworthy. Every reader of the Quarterly Statement of the Palestine Exploration Fund is familiar with the controversy on Jerusalem topography. The disputants are all keen students of the Bible and of the locality. They are set on labelling every hill, valley, edifice, and watercourse with its Biblical name. Why is it that they cannot agree ? Simply because the Scripture gives scattered hints concerning localities familiar to the writers, but supplies no formal description such as can be found in Josephus. Any such description would be foreign to the purpose of the Sacred Books.

CHAPTER XX.

LEGISLATIVE CODES IN THE PENTATEUCH.

1. The question of the composition of the Pentateuch is *Origin of Biblical legislation.* usually discussed in connection with two subjects—the legis- lative enactments which pass under the name of Moses, and the use of the name Jehovah. We have now to consider the first of these subjects.

Taking the Pentateuch as it stands, we find that it contains stages of law or regulation answering to the development of social and national life. There was law, in its fundamental and initial stage, in Paradise. It consisted of the principle of obedience to the voice of the Creator, in Whose image man had been formed, and Who had the right to demand submission from his children. Along with this principle we find indications of a marriage law, an industrial law, and a Sabbath law. After the Fall, through the breach of a specific regulation, human passion was let loose, and evil culminated at the period of the Flood; some additional elementary legislation, bearing on the preservation of life, being subsequently introduced. All law in these early stages is regarded as from God, and is accompanied with promises and penalties. During the Patriarchal age we find custom growing up into law, *e.g.* with reference to the purchase of property and of personal service, the claim of the firstborn, the binding nature of oaths and covenants, the rule of betrothal, and the raising up of seed to a brother (commonly called the levirate law, from an old Latin word *levir*, which signifies brother-in-law).

2. We pass from the Patriarchal to the Mosaic age, when *The Mosaic Law.* Israel became a redeemed people, and thus in a new sense bound to obey God. This principle lies at the root of all

further legislation, and is traceable throughout the Penta-teuch, no motive of a later date being set forth.

Modern criticism has done good service in calling atten-tion to the fact that the last four Books of Moses contain different codes. These may be taken in the order in which they occur. It may be mentioned in passing that the word *Torah,* usually translated Law, means guidance rather than legislation, and indicates that the principles of Divine legis-lation are like a father's voice, intended to guide his children into the right way. It first occurs in Gen. **26. 5,** and is generally used of the whole Mosaic legislation, ceremonial or otherwise, whether uttered by mouth (*e.g.* Deut. **1. 5**), or written (Deut. **29. 21** ; 1 Kings **2. 3**), or expounded by the priests (2 Chron. **15. 3** ; Hag. **2. 11** ; Mal. **2. 7**).

Ten Com-mandments. First come the Ten Commandments, which constituted the original Covenant between God and Israel.

Exod. 21-23. The second series of legal enactments—or, as they are called, " judgments "—will be found in Exod. **21-23.** They have to do with the rights of persons and property, which are dealt with from a religious point of view. Some of them were prospective, but the larger number were applicable to the wilderness life. They are preceded by a rule for building altars (Exod. **20. 22-26**), which was for immediate and general observance ; and they are followed by a promise and a warning concerning life in Canaan, which the people were supposed to be entering shortly.

Exod. 34. A few weeks later bring us to another code, very much shorter than the first, emphasizing the religious rather than the social enactments (Exod. **34**).

The Leviti-cal code. The directions for the structure of the Tabernacle in Exodus are rubrical and symbolical, and a considerable part of Leviticus is ceremonial and preparatory, being based on old sacrificial custom, and abounding in ritual details, which would tend, if obeyed, to keep the religious observances of Israel free from heathen superstitions. When, however, we get to the 19th and six following chapters of Leviticus, we find the social element re-appearing. The 26th chapter contains highly developed promises and threats, and the chapter closes with a summary which indicates that the whole is regarded as one code or body of legislation. It professedly dates from Sinai and from the beginning of the second year of wilderness life, and was arranged with a view to the immediate occupation of Palestine. There is nothing which in itself bears the mark of a late date in this department of law.

Forty (or, strictly speaking, thirty-eight) years of wilderness seclusion followed, and during this time the various codes, which must have been recorded at the time of their being issued, lay in the priests' keeping, together with the Patriarchal documents. The earlier part of the Book of Numbers consists of camp regulations, and the few enactments which are found in the middle and at the close of the Book of Numbers grew up in the course of this period, and are developments and re-adjustments of the earlier laws. *Camp regulations.*

3. The speeches in the Book of Deuteronomy, in which the aged leader reviews the history and legislation of the past, are in fair accordance with the contents of the three preceding books. The Ten Words re-appear with homiletic insertions, and Moses points out that they were followed by certain statutes and judgments, though he does not enumerate them (Deut. **5.** 31, 32). It is only when we get to the 12th chapter that Moses begins to repeat the actual laws of past days, and we gather from the eighth verse that they had been to a great extent ignored by the people hitherto. Moses is not at this stage making laws but preaching, pointing out the original principles which were laid down at the Exodus, giving verbal extracts from the early bye-laws, and illustrating by instances with which the Wanderings had made the people familiar, as when he adds to the list of clean and unclean creatures some names with which they had only become acquainted in the wilderness. *Speeches in Deuteronomy.*

The variations and additions which may be noted on comparing Deuteronomy with the previous books are chiefly in the way of modification, adaptation, and growth. They intimate that we have not to do with a cast-iron code, but with rules for life; and it is important to observe that they are all from the lips of Moses himself; so that the person who was appointed to begin the work of legislation was enabled to finish it. They present us with a strong proof of the antiquity of the books; for later writers would have given us a systematic code, such as Josephus attempted to draw up. As the books stand, history is interwoven with legislation, and episodes are mingled with enactments, so that we have a natural growth, not an artificial compound.

Special features of the book. It is important to notice how Moses, in this last book, made provision for the future. He contemplated the time when the people would be settled in Canaan, when there would be a fixed habitation of God in the land, and when there would be a king over Israel. He pointed to the priests and judges as the expounders of the mind of God and of the book which was in their charge. He predicted that at some future time another Prophet should rise whose Word must be strictly attended to. Lastly, he re-affirms the promises and threats of Lev. **26** (see Deut. **28–30**); teaches the people the great song which contained an outline of the future (Deut. **32**); blesses the tribes in terms very different from those of Jacob, and yet with a marked reference to Jacob's blessing in the case of Joseph (Deut. **33**); commits the charge of Israel to his faithful follower Joshua; and resigns his spirit to God.

Difficulty in Mosaic legislation. 4. It is allowed by most critics that the variations in the laws as given in the earlier and later Mosaic books do not present insuperable difficulties. But what they have specially felt about the Mosaic legislation is, that it seems inconsistent with the subsequent history of the people. It seems to a large extent ideal, and to have been practically ignored, not only by the people, but even by the early prophets, and it came upon everybody quite as a surprise in the days of Josiah; consequently the more advanced critics regard it as an invention of different ages and parties, intended to bolster up priestcraft; whilst the more moderate consider that it is a growth, having originated orally (and to some extent perhaps in writing) in the days of Moses, and having been added to in the time of Jeremiah, and in a later period.

There appears, however, to be no necessity for adopting either of these views. We have shown in previous papers that there are references to Mosaic laws and institutions all the way through the Historical Books, and that Deuteronomy is quoted *verbatim* in the Book of Kings. What more is needed? We could hardly expect such brief sketches of long periods as we possess in the Judges to bristle with quotations from the Law.

5. Still, it is answered, if the Pentateuch had been in *A further difficulty.* existence in the days of the judges and early kings the course of things would have been different; the Levitical system would have been more carefully adhered to; and the prophets would have set themselves more carefully to the task of rebuking the people for the breach of definite laws. This last is a matter of some importance. It would seem that the prophets had direct messages from God, beyond which they did not often go, and that the priests shut their eyes and ears to what was unpleasant. Politics overshadowed religion. Heathenism overwhelmed Mosaic ceremonial. The written records were kept, but not acted upon as a whole. Certain portions were familiar to the priest, and still more modest extracts were known to the people, but the rest was practically a dead letter. Incense might be offered to the brazen serpent; high-places dedicated by king Solomon to Ashtoreth, Chemosh, and Milcom ; horses might be given to the Sun by the kings of Judah, and placed at the entering in of the House of the Lord; and either no one protested, or, if they did, they were silenced and slain. None of these things prove the non-existence of the Law, but they reflect gross discredit on the priesthood; and they make it impossible for us to believe that the later priests could have invented any of

the Pentateuch codes and attributed them to Moses, stamping thereby their own predecessors with everlasting disgrace.

Analogy with Christian legislation.

6. The case is somewhat, though not altogether, similar to that of the New Testament. Our Lord legislated for the future. A large part of His legislation, *e.g.* the Sermon on the Mount, contemplated a state of things which we have never yet seen carried out. Much of the New Testament teaching was gradually ignored and finally superseded by a debased religion. The finding of the Law by Hilkiah is like the reading of the Bible by Martin Luther, and a Reformation followed in each case, tending to bring men back to the study of the earlier documents. It cannot be denied that the Mosaic legislation was practically to a large extent a failure, but theologically it gives us a hopeful ideal. The same is true of Christianity to some extent. The adherents of this religion of peace keep millions of soldiers ready for war, and the professed followers of One Who impoverished Himself and sacrificed Himself, accumulate wealth and live selfish, luxurious lives. It is not to be forgotten, however, that in each case downfall follows on neglect of law, whilst prosperity is granted to those who return to God and abide by His written law. This may be illustrated both from the prophetic chapters of the Pentateuch and from all the histories which follow.

Origin and use of ceremonial laws.

7. It is unnecessary for our present purpose to inquire how far the laws given by Moses were of Patriarchal origin, or what Egyptian or Arab elements they incorporated. National habits, whether religious or social, cannot easily be broken down, and the Law had to be adapted to the hardness of the people's hearts, both in what it permitted and in what it forbade. We are all indebted to Moses for his setting forth of moral and social laws, and even for his ceremonial legislation, much of which is in accordance with the very latest discoveries of science.*

---

* This was pointed out in a paper in the *Contemporary Review* by the late Mr. G. S. Drew some years ago ; see also *Nineteenth Century*, September, 1889.

It is a question, however, whether the people ever obeyed the letter of the Law or put in force the penalties which are imposed therein, many of which, it should be observed, are far more stringent than would have been admitted in a later legislation, whilst others were only adapted to camp life.

8. A question may fairly be raised whether reformers, such as existed in the days of David, Josiah, and Nehemiah, have incorporated later laws into the Books of Moses. We *Are there interpolations?* know that David made numerous regulations, bye-laws, and ordinances, bearing not only on the civil interests of the people but also on the work of the priests and Levites, and that he committed these new rules to writing. (See 1 Chron. **23**. 27; 2 Chron. **23**. 18; **35**. 4.) But they appear to have been matters of administration rather than of legislation, and were doubtless kept within Mosaic lines. When Moses ordered that no one should add to or take from the words of the Law (Deut. **4**. 2; **12**. 32), he was specially referring to the danger of compromise with heathenism, and some students think that the statute book was not absolutely closed by these utterances. If so we could readily understand, from the analogous history of the Christian Liturgy, how the substance of a legislation might remain unchanged, yet rubrical directions issued under proper authority might accumulate. But we have no record of such a thing having been done in the case of the Pentateuch, and to suppose that it was done surreptitiously in the days of Josiah, Nehemiah, or later, is to create a moral difficulty, and that without due reason. There are no marks of late legal insertions in the Pentateuch, whether literary or historical. As the Dean of Canterbury has lately pointed out (*Churchman*, June, 1890), the codes are all in the same old Hebrew style, and to make them the creation of various ages is to create fresh linguistic as well as moral difficulties. The presumption is thus strongly in favour of the whole being the work of Moses.

CHAPTER XXI.

SPECIAL OFFICES AND ORDINANCES.

Names of officials in Old Testament.

1. There is a strong official element in the Old Testament, partly civil and partly religious. It gathers to a large extent round two central names, Moses and David. It involves the use of a great many terms, some of which are quite peculiar, their origin being at present unknown, though further research will probably bring them to light. The English language is not adapted to reproduce all these peculiarities, but the critic is bound to examine them. He will inquire whether the Hebrew writers are consistent in their use of certain terms for certain things, and will consider their bearing on the age and condition of the books. A few instances will illustrate the class of words referred to.

Titles of rulers.

2. Whilst only one word stands for " king " all through the Old Testament (מֶלֶךְ), whether he be an emperor or a sheikh, there is a peculiar word for " queen " in certain passages (גְבִירָה), which is never used till the Book of Kings, while the masculine form of it (גְבִיר) is only used of Jacob's lordship over Esau (Gen. **27.** 29, 37). There are sixteen Hebrew words translated " prince " in the Old Testament, the most ordinary being the word *Sar* (שַׂר), the root of which is found in the name Israel; but the feminine form *Sarah* occurs for the first time (except as the name of Abraham's wife) in Judg. **5.** 29, where it is used of the Canaanite ladies; and in the four other passages where the word is found there is a foreign air about it (see 1 Kings **11.** 3; Esth. **1.** 18; Isa. **49.** 23; Lam. **1.** 1). Thirteen Hebrew words are translated " governor." One of them (חָקַק) occurs in Judg. **5.** 9 and 14 only in this sense,

being usually rendered "lawgiver," and originally meaning
one who depicts or engraves (a decree). It is curious that
the same word in a slightly different form is found in the
15th verse, where the A. V. translates "*thoughts*" (marg.
impressions) of heart." The English word "duke" stands
for *Nasic* (נָסִיךְ) in Josh. **13**. 21 with respect to the associated chiefs under Sihon, king of the Amorites, and is only
used elsewhere for foreign princes, unless Mic. **5**. 5 be an
exception; in other passages the word "duke" stands for
Aluph (אַלּוּף), which is only applied to the rulers of Edom
(Gen. **36**; Exod. **15**; 1 Chron. **1**), until we reach Zechariah,
where it is used of governors of Judah (Zech. **9**. 7; **12**. 5, 6).
A special word (סֶרֶן) is used of the "lords" of the Philis
tines wherever they are referred to, *i.e.* in Joshua, Judges,
Samuel, and Chronicles. The word "chief" does duty for
sixteen Hebrew words, including the remarkable word (נָצַח)
translated "chief musician," and some peculiar words in
Samuel, such as the feminine word פִּנָּה, which originally
means "corner," and is used of influential Israelites in
Judg. **20**. 2, and 1 Sam. **14**. 38. Under the English word
"officer" we find the *Saris* (סָרִיס), or eunuch, a word used
both of Egyptian and Oriental officers from Genesis to
Daniel. A special word (נָצָב) is used in 1 Kings **4**. 7, and
in 2 Chron. **8**. 10, with respect to some of Solomon's officials,
who are regarded as "pillars" of the state. It is also used
of the "deputy" over Edom, 1 Kings **22**. 47, and of the
servant *set over* the reapers in Ruth **2**. 5, 6; but never
before, though the root itself is common enough. Another
word translated "officer" is familiar to us in the form
"sultan." It is fairly frequent in the later books, but never
used in the early books except of Joseph's governorship
over Egypt (Gen. **42**. 6). Another peculiar word is used in
Exodus, Deuteronomy, Joshua, and Chronicles only (and in
Prov. **6**. 7), viz., *Shotar* (שֹׁטֵר). It may possibly be of Egyptian origin, but is only used of Israelite officials. *See* p. 29.

We need not refer to the titles of officers in the different
departments established by David and Solomon, but must

point out that a number of official titles are used in the later books, such as pasha, noble, satrap, chancellor, the tirshatha, sheshbazzar, which are never found in the earlier books.

It will be seen from this brief notice that the subject is not a trifling one, and that there was plenty of room for a later editor to make a slip in composing or revising books professedly of an early date; but we do not find such slips, and the evidence goes in favour of the traditional view.

Office of priest.

3. Turning from secular to sacred titles our attention is called to the word *cohen* (כֹּהֵן), which is translated "priest" in almost all places in the Old Testament. It is of uncertain origin,* and was not always used of a minister in things pertaining to God. It is consistently used of heathen priests as well as of the Israelite priesthood, except in 2 Kings **23. 5,** and Hos. **10. 5.** The office was a growth from Patriarchal and pre-Patriarchal times, and lay with the head of a family or his representative. Even after the Exodus each tribe had its own priests (Exod. **29. 22–24**), and it is not likely that this ancient system of tribal priests was entirely done away with even when a special family was singled out by God for the performance of religious functions. The selection of the tribe of Levi as a sacred hereditary caste, and of the family of Aaron as the ministers of the Sanctuary, caused offence among the people, and brought about the circumstances narrated in Num. **16–18.** The Appendix to the Book of Judges, chaps. **17–21,** reveals a strange state of things. Some of the people were still in a semi-heathenish condition, and clung to their old debased religious system, even though they had the Ark of the Covenant, and Phinehas ministering at it (Judg. **20.** 27, 28).

"The priests the Levites."

4. Attention has been frequently directed to an expression which we find in certain books. A distinction is drawn in the time of Ezekiel (chap. **44.** 10–16) between the Levites who were to minister and "the priests the Levites" who

---

* See the discussion on the word in *Old Testament Synonyms.*

were to offer. Some have imagined that this is a late distinction; but is this supposition necessary? In the rubrical directions of Leviticus and in Numbers we read of the priest, the anointed priest, and Aaron's sons the priests. In Deuteronomy, and once in Joshua, we come across the expression "the priests the Levites." Why is this used? Is it not to distinguish the Levitical priests from the Tribal priests spoken of above? This seems natural enough. There is no reason and no need for bringing down either the expression or the books that use it to the age of Ezekiel. Books cannot be shifted to and fro on such a slender hypothesis as this. In 1 Kings 8. 4, which is comparatively early, we read of "the priests and the Levites." In Isa. 66. 21, which we take to be written in the time of Manasseh, but which some critics take to be much later, we read of some being taken "for priests for Levites," the *and* in the A. V. and R. V. being in italics. In the Chronicles, which is comparatively late, we have both expressions used close together (2 Chron. 30. 25, 27). In 1 Kings 12. 31 we are told (R. V.) that Jeroboam "made priests from among all the people which were not of the sons of Levi," thus returning to the Tribal priesthood which Moses, under Divine direction, had sought to curtail.

It seems clear, on the whole, that the expression "the priests the Levites" simply means "the Levitical priests" as opposed to the non-Levitical or Tribal priests, and that it has no bearing whatever on the dates of the books.

5. The land tenure of the priestly family was totally *Land tenure* different from that of the other tribes. It is referred to *of priests.* again and again in the Pentateuch, Joshua, and the Chronicles. Although, however, the priests and Levites had special lands allotted to them, there was no law forbidding them to live and acquire territory in other parts of the country. In Josh. 24. 33 we are told that Eleazar died, and they buried him in a hill which pertaineth to Phinehas his son, which was given him in Mount Ephraim. He was of

K

course a Kohathite, and we find in Josh. **21** that the Kohathites had cities in Ephraim; yet, being of Aaron's family, his
proper locality was not in Ephraim but further south (compare Josh. **21**. 4, 5). Samuel was a Kohathite, according
to the two genealogies which we have of him in 1 Chron. **6**,
but not an Aaronite; so that his family were rightly
located in Mount Ephraim (1 Sam. **1**. 1). But the Ephraimite cities allotted to the Kohathites in Josh. **21**. 20–22
do not include Ramah, where Samuel and his father lived.
It seems strange that anyone should doubt Samuel's descent
merely because his father or one of his forefathers is called
an Ephrathite (*i.e.* according to the usual interpretation, an
Ephraimite). He was, strictly speaking, an Ephrathite Kohathite, the one word marking his locality and the other his
descent. Strange to say, Professor Driver, in his useful and
painstaking work on the text of Samuel, departs from his
usual caution, and creates a " discrepancy " between the Book
of Samuel (which we doubtless have from Samuel himself)
and the Books of Chronicles (which we possibly owe in part
to Samuel's descendants), and suggests that " Samuel was
really of Ephraimite descent, and was only in later times
reckoned as a Levite." He thus throws overboard, without the slightest necessity, the two semi-independent genealogies of Samuel's family in 1 Chron. **6**, makes Heman
the grandson of Samuel a genealogical impostor, and casts
doubt on the honesty of the genealogies generally as far
back as the days of the Exodus, where we are first
introduced to the name Elkanah in the family of Korah
(Exod. **6**. 24).

High-
places.

6. Much has been written about the HIGH-PLACES in
Palestine. We must evidently draw a distinction between
two classes which originally existed side by side. The
Patriarchs set up altars wherever they worshipped God, and
probably they were on the hills, worship being then con-
ducted in the open air. When Israel re-entered Canaan it
would be natural that they should have numerous centres

of worship, and that they should feel specially attached to
the sacred places of their ancestors at Shechem, Bethel,
Hebron, and elsewhere. But the Canaanites also had their
altars and high-places, and the danger would be that Israel
should worship at these, and so be led into adopting heathenish rites. Accordingly, the Law ordered that all Canaanite
high-places should be destroyed (Num. **33**. 52). But did it
forbid all worship whatsoever except at one place? That
would be a strange regulation. It is clear, on the one hand,
that Moses predicts the establishment of a great religious
centre where God's Name should be specially honoured; and
Solomon refers to this fact when he dedicates the Temple;
but it is not equally clear that all local worship was for-
bidden.

7. There are, indeed, no special orders in the Law con- *Altars.*
cerning the setting up of local sanctuaries; in fact there
are no orders about prayer at all. The allusions to "sanctuaries" in Lev. **26**. 31 and **21**. 23 are not sufficient to found
any argument upon. But there can hardly be any doubt
that not only in the Levitical cities, but also wherever there
was a gathering of people, some kind of worship would be
carried on. The remarkable narrative concerning the altar
constructed on the east of the Jordan (Josh. **22**) does not
militate against this conclusion. There was fear lest it
should be a centre of worship in the same sense that the
Tabernacle was, and this was not to be allowed. Any such
rival system would have been destructive of Israelitish unity.
Altars were tacitly sanctioned in the age of the Judges
(Judg. **6**. 24); and in the time of Samuel, who did so much
to put down Baal-worship, altars are freely referred to, and
high-places also (see 1 Sam. **7**. 17; **9**. 12; **13**. 10; **14**. 35).
Some of these high-places had some edifices connected with
them, which could serve as hiding-places (1 Sam. **13**. 6).
The altars of Samaria which were thrown down by Ahab
and others (1 Kings **19**. 10) were not heathen altars; and
the altar on Carmel which Elijah rebuilt was not a heathen

K 2

one. These were relics of ancient days, and had been a natural provision for local worship all through Israel's history.

8. We cannot close the discussion of legislation without referring to the feasts and ritual solemnities ordained by Moses. Some of these, as the Sabbath, marriage, and circumcision, were old ordinances. Other religious customs connected with sacrifice, the priesthood, prayer, washings, blessing and cursing, oaths, tithes, and burial, seem to have been a common inheritance amongst ancient nations. Certain great ordinances sprang out of incidents in Israelite history, *e.g.* the Passover, the Feast of Tabernacles, and possibly the Pentecost, which may have been connected with the giving of the Law. The origin of these feasts and solemnities is given in the early books. It has been observed that the references to them in the later books are few and far between, and sometimes doubtful. The argument from silence in such a case is a very unsafe one. This may be illustrated from the fact that the custom concerning the sinew (Gen. **32**. 32), the fringe (Num. **15**. 39), and the lamentation over Jephthah's daughter (Judg. **11**. 40), are never named after the account of their origin. Even the Passover is only once referred to in the second half of the Old Testament. Again, it must not be forgotten that the Israelites were peculiarly tenacious in matters of custom. Can it be imagined that a series of solemnities would have been sprung upon them in the days of Josiah or Ezra as of Mosaic origin? Or can it be imagined that some priest devised them (as Jeroboam is said to have invented a feast, 1 Kings **12**. 32), and persuaded the people that they were ancient?

Some critics have suggested that there was only one feast originally, viz., " the yearly feast in Shiloh " (Judg. **21**. 19; 1 Sam. **1**. 3, 21), so that the orders in Exod. **23**. 14 and Deut. **16**. 16, commanding the people to go up three times a year, were of later origin. But apply this hypothesis to the

New Testament. We are told in Luke **2.** 41 that our Lord's parents went up yearly to the Feast of the Passover. Are we to gather from this that the Pentecost and Tabernacle Feasts had not yet been ordained? The truth is that the word translated " yearly " in Judges and Samuel simply means "periodical," and does not specify how often the festive occasions would arise; and probably, as a matter of fact, during the dead period which followed Joshua's decease, the people did very much what was right in their own eyes, following Moses in part and yielding to other traditional and heathenish influences where it was most convenient. That this was the case in the matter of the Sabbatical year we are plainly told in 2 Chron. **36.** 21 ; and this is only a sample of that negligence which is to be seen all through the Jewish history, and which can be sadly paralleled in the records of Christendom.

CHAPTER XXII.

NAMES OF GOD IN THE OLD TESTAMENT.

Discussion of the Divine names. 1. The Old Testament is the nursery-ground of New Testament theology. The mission of Christ is a mission from God, and is intended to bring men back to God. The revelation of God contained in the Old Testament is presupposed throughout the New. The invisible Father of our spirits, Himself a Spirit, Who cannot lie, the blessed and only Potentate, the Father of lights, from Whom all good gifts come, Who spoke in times past by the prophets, hath now spoken by His Son. There is a continuity of spiritual impressions and spiritual actions all through the Bible, and the spring of them all is the living GOD.

In discussing the use of the names of God in the Old Testament the student is conscious of a certain painful hesitation. If we had to criticize books in which the titles and work of our own parents were discussed, we should shrink from a free bandying about of their revered names. The Biblical critic is in danger of regarding the titles of his God and Father as if they were so many counters. May we be preserved from a barren and irreverent spirit of criticism whilst inquiring into the facts concerning the sacred names of Him in Whom we live, and move, and have our being.

Variety in the names. 2. It must be noticed, in the first place, that we find several distinct though related titles given to God in the Old Testament. Some are very general in their meaning, *e.g.* the word LORD (אֲדֹנָי, *Adonai*), which signifies "master" or "owner," exactly answering to the Greek κύριος, and applicable to man as well as to God. The word generally translated GOD is *Elohim* (אֱלֹהִים), which occurs 2,555 times in the Old Testament; in 2,310 places it is used of the true God, and in the other passages it has secondary or heathen applications.*

Other titles are somewhat more specific in the idea which they convey, *e.g.* the name *Shaddai* (שַׁדַּי), usually found with *El*, and generally translated, after Jerome, ALMIGHTY. Another title to be ranked with it is the Most High (עֶלְיוֹן, *'Elion*). Whilst one of these marks God's bountifulness and all-sufficiency, the other indicates His exaltation.

3. Secondly, we find tendencies in certain writers to use one of these titles rather than another. Thus *Shaddai* is specially used in Job; the same is the case with *Eloah*, which is usually reckoned an Aramaic form. *Elah* is found no less than thirty-seven times in the short Book of Ezra, and forty-six times in Daniel, being only found in one other passage; it is thus associated with Chaldee. The short word *El* is specially to be found in Job, the Psalms, and Isaiah, being used (as *Elah*, *Eloah*, and *Elohim* are) not only of the One living and true God, but also of the gods of the heathen. *Tendencies in writers.*

4. We must now concentrate our attention on one title of God, which is recognized as the most national of all— the name JEHOVAH. The origin of this name is lost in mystery. How was it originally pronounced? What does it mean? Who first used it or heard it uttered? The subject on which we are engaged does not make it necessary for us to discuss the first of these questions. Out of deference to ancient custom we propose to adhere to the old pronunciation, as given above, rather than to the more critical JAHVEH. We take JEHOVAH, or its shorter form JAH, to be the personal name of the God of Israel from the time *The name Jehovah.*

---

* I may be permitted to refer for full details on this subject to a work on *Old Testament Synonyms*, published some years ago by Messrs. Longman.

of the Exodus onwards. It stands alone in its glory; it permits of no definite article in front of it, nor of any suffix after it; it is never used of any false god, nor in the plural number.

English version.

We lose some of the force of this title by having followed the LXX. in translating it THE LORD. Thus when Moses and Aaron went to Pharaoh they said, "Thus saith Jehovah the God of Israel," and Pharaoh answered, "Who is Jehovah that I should obey His voice?" (see Exod. 5. 1, 2). Jehovah is the chief Speaker and Actor all through the rest of the history of Israel. He is not regarded as one of a pantheon, but as the living and eternal Being to Whom all creation owes existence, and Who had chosen Israel to Himself as a special people. Although the word LORD is printed in small capitals in our Authorized Old Testament when it stands for the name "Jehovah," yet readers do not always observe it, and of course hearers cannot tell when this name is used and when the word "Lord" stands for the title *Adonai*. The change between the titles is frequent and subtle. Thus, in Exod. 5. 22 we read, "Moses returned unto the LORD, and said, Lord, wherefore hast Thou evil intreated this people?" Here the printing in the A. V. shows that Moses returned to Jehovah and appealed to Him as his Master. (Compare 1 Kings 3. 5, "Jehovah appeared to Solomon, and God said"—also verses 10, 11. See also Isa. 6. 1, 3, 5, 8.)

Usage of the name.

After the first few chapters in Exodus, Jehovah is the name specially used for the Deliverer. In Leviticus hardly any other word is used, except in relation to Jehovah, as in the expression "Jehovah your God." The same is true of Numbers, except in the episode concerning Balaam. We find the same mode of expression in the rest of the Historical Books down to the time of Nehemiah.

Its origin.

5. We now wish to get back to the origin of the word. Two passages in Exodus are of special importance. It is, of course, useless to look at them unless we can trust them,

but critics of all schools seem to have regarded them as a trustworthy basis for discussion.

In Exod. **3** Moses gives us his own account of the vision of the burning bush, and—as the narrator—uses the title Jehovah freely. He tells how the angel of Jehovah appeared (verse 2) ; how when Jehovah saw him turn aside God called (verse 4), and revealed Himself as the *Elohim* of the Patriarchs. Thus Moses was conscious that he was in a visionary condition, the spiritual sense of hearing having been specially quickened, so that he was brought into communion with the God of his ancestors ; and he hid his face, for he was afraid to look upon God (verse 6). After receiving his commission he puts this important question : " When I come to the children of Israel, and say, The God of your fathers hath sent me unto you ; and they shall say, What is His name ? what shall I say unto them ? " Does this imply that Israel had no specific name for their God ? or that they had more than one ? Let us see the answer. " God said to Moses, I AM THAT I AM: and He said, Thus shall ye say to the children of Israel, I AM hath sent me unto you. And God said further unto Moses, Thus shalt thou say to the children of Israel, JEHOVAH the God of your fathers, the God of Abraham, of Isaac, and of Jacob, hath appeared to me." This last sentence seems to imply that Abraham, Isaac, and Jacob were familiar names to Israel, and that their God was named JEHOVAH. There would be no doubt of this conclusion in any mind were it not for the existence of another passage, which seems at first sight to lead to an opposite view. On turning to Exod. **6. 3** we find. God speaking again to Moses, and saying, " I am JEHOVAH, and I appeared unto Abraham, unto Isaac, and unto Jacob, by (the name of) EL SHADDAI ; but (as regards) my name JEHOVAH, I was not known to them." What can this mean ? Does it really signify that the name Jehovah had never been heard by the Patriarchs ? that it was never used till the Exodus ? and that on the strength of this honest account of Moses' interview with God we are to conclude

Exod. 3.

Exod. 6. 3.

that the name Jehovah when it occurs in Genesis must be a Mosaic or post-Mosaic insertion? This would at first be a natural conclusion; but it is not a certain one, being in flat contradiction to that already drawn from Exod. 3. Besides, Moses must have known the name of his own mother. How could he calmly tell us that his mother's name was Jochebed (*i.e.* the glory of Jah) if the name Jah or Jehovah was not uttered until her son was eighty years old?

Possible solution of difficulty. Another case may help us out of the difficulty. In 1 Sam. 3. 7 we read, "Now Samuel did not yet know Jehovah, neither was the word of Jehovah yet revealed unto him." This cannot mean that Samuel had never heard the name Jehovah, with which, indeed, he must have been quite familiar; but it must signify some special knowledge of Him.

Now let us suppose that in the days of the Patriarchs the name of Jehovah was specially associated with covenants and promises, and that the name itself signifies primarily One Who *is*, and hence One Who is eternal and true to His word; then we can readily understand how much greater significance would be attached to this name in consequence of the events connected with the Exodus, since this was itself a fulfilment of the promise made to the Patriarchs.

We do not, however, wish to press this solution. The difficulty has been felt in past ages quite as much as to-day. Theoretically it is quite possible that Moses, whom we take to be the authorizer, if not the editor, of Genesis, may have substituted the name Jehovah for other titles in the Patriarchal narrative, just as the writer of Chronicles has taken the opposite course, frequently substituting the name Elohim for Jehovah in the narratives which he extracts from Samuel and Kings. It will be well, however, before deciding the matter, to look back a little further.

Names of God in Genesis. 6. The Book of Genesis is the true and original birthplace of all theology. It contains those ideas of God and man, of

righteousness and judgment, of responsibility and moral
government, of failure and hope, which are presupposed
through the rest of the Old Testament, and which prepare
the way for the mission of Christ. Most of the names and
titles of God are to be found in its pages, though some few
are later, as the Chaldean *Elah*, and the striking title "the
LORD of Hosts," which does not appear till Samuel. We
find the most general of all names, *Elohim*, in the first verse
of the Bible associated with creation. The form of the word
is plural, though it governs a verb which is in the singular
number. The singular form, *Eloah*, does not appear till
Deut. **32.** 15. Again we find *El* introduced in the Patriarchal
age (Gen. **14.** 18, &c.), and *El* is found in composition with
Elohim in Gen. **32.** 30 (El-Elohe-Israel). So we find
Shaddai formally revealed as a title of God, in connection
with *El*, in Gen. **17.** 1, "I am the Almighty God; walk
before Me, and be thou perfect." It is here associated with
a special promise of the multiplication of seed, as also in the
next two passages where it occurs (Gen. **28.** 3 and **35.** 11).
There are two other passages where it is found in Genesis,
viz., chap. **43.** 14 and **49.** 25, both of which awaken the
thought of God's bounty and grace. The familiar title
Adonai, "Lord," is first found in Gen. **15.** 2, 8. If anyone
will trace its usage through the early books of the Bible, he
will find that it is almost, if not quite, confined to prayers
or addresses to God, Who is regarded as the Owner, Master,
and Governor of the world. It is associated where it first
occurs, and in several later passages, with the name Jehovah.
The title *'Elion*, "Most High," is first found in Gen. **14.** 18,
in the account of Melchizedek. It does not occur again till
the time of Balaam, and afterwards it is confined to poetry,
being specially found in the Psalms.

It will be observed that all these names are threaded
together, *El* with *Shaddai* and *'Elion*, *Jehovah* with
Elohim and with *Adonai*, *Elohim* with *El*. We have no
pantheon here, but aspects of One self-revealing God, "the
living God," as Joshua and others called Him; "the God

of the spirits of all flesh," as Moses called Him; "the Possessor of heaven and earth," as Melchizedek called Him.

The question re-stated. 7. So much in illustration of what has been pointed out above, viz., that Genesis is the true spring-head of the Divine titles and of the ideas which they embody. Have we, however, any reason for drawing a line round the name Jehovah wherever it occurs in Genesis, so as to indicate that either the name or the passages which contain it are post-Mosaic?

Analogy with names of Christ. There seems to be a reason, at any rate in the older books, for the use of one name rather than another for God, even though in later days it may not have been so. The comparative usage of " Jesus " and " Christ " in the New Testament affords us a convenient analogy, and there is no more reason in the nature of things for dividing out the Book of Genesis amongst several writers according to their use of one or other name for God than for parcelling out various sections of St. Paul's Epistles on a similar ground.

Use of name Jehovah in Genesis. 8. The name *Jehovah* first comes on the scene in Genesis 2. 4, when the creative *Elohim* enters into definite communication with man. The keynote is thus given to Biblical theology. Such expressions as " the word of Jehovah " and " the angel of Jehovah " spring out of the fact recorded in the second of Genesis that the Lord of heaven and earth has laid a peculiar responsibility on man, and has made special provisions for his welfare. The first Jehovah-section runs from Gen. 2. 4 to chap. 3. 24; but it is noticeable that the serpent does not use this name. In Gen. 4. 1–26 the writer uses the name Jehovah without adding Elohim (which is found with it in the previous section), and special attention is given to the name in the last verse, where we read, " Then began men to call upon the name of Jehovah." The time referred to is when Seth's son Enos was born. The Revisers have not altered the translation, but they have struck out the alternative rendering contained in our margins (" or to call themselves by the name of," &c.). This decision is important, as it bears upon many passages in the Old and New Testament. The passage cited looks like a piece of pre-Mosaic traditional history. It would imply that in this early stage of human history there was an idea of God which the Hebrew JEHOVAH best expresses, and this idea was the basis of prayer. In other words, people prayed not to Elohim as such, but to Elohim as revealed in the faithful Promiser, Who all through the later Hebrew line of tradition was known as Jehovah.

It is needless to analyse the whole of Genesis. Speaking shortly, we find the name Elohim in Gen. **5**. 1–32, variations in chaps. **6–9**, Jehovah in chaps. **11–14**, and variations between the two names in the later chapters. It seems as unreasonable as it is unnecessary to suppose that either the name Jehovah was inserted in the old documents by Moses, or that the documents themselves were post-Mosaic.

9. The theory that there were different narratives, tradi- *Are there different documents?* tional and written, some tending to emphasise the name Jehovah, and others content with the title Elohim, is in itself quite unobjectionable, and commends itself to many minds. But it has led to so many unnatural splittings-up of the text that it must be received with great reserve. If, as we have attempted to show in earlier pages, Moses is the compiler or authorizer of the main body of Genesis, then the various documents out of which he composed the book may have represented various theological impressions, and may have contained various titles, some, perhaps, Accadian, or even pre-Babel, and he may have been led to use the mysterious name Jehovah as a translation or substitute for some more ancient title found in the primæval materials with which he had to deal. This is, however, pure speculation.

It is doubtful if there were collateral documents in those *Difficulty of this theory.* ancient days analogous with those from which the Chronicles were compiled. There may have been some; but the multiplication of imaginary documents will often lead to the multiplication of real difficulties. Have we, for example, two documents in Gen. **21.** 1–6, where we read that "Jehovah visited Sarah, as He had said, and Sarah said, Elohim hath made me to laugh"? Have we not, rather, Jehovah introduced as the faithful Promiser, and Elohim as the forceful Worker? Again, in verse 33, "Abraham called on the name of Jehovah, the eternal *El*": did one document use the one expression, and another give the second? In the 22nd chapter Elohim tempts Abraham, and, when questioned by his son, the Patriarch replies, "Elohim will provide," but the place is called "Jehovah will provide." In chap. **24.** 7 Abraham calls Jehovah the Elohim of heaven and earth, manifestly referring to creation, and then describes the Divine Promise, which accounts for the name Jehovah being subsequently introduced. In chap. **26.** 24 Jehovah appears to Isaac, and says, "I am the Elohim of Abraham thy father," and proceeds to give him a further promise. Is it necessary, is it critical, to invent two or three semi-independent writers in order to produce such a verse as this? Is it not far simpler and more reasonable to take the view that Elohim sets forth God as the putter forth of force, whilst Jehovah sets Him forth as the speaker to the spirit and the faithful Promiser?

Conclusion. 10. There are many perplexities still remaining which will occur to every student. Why, for example, did Jacob so rarely use the name Jehovah, and Joseph not at all? The reason may be discernible, but we must be content with a general conclusion, namely, that either the name Jehovah was in use in primæval times, or it has replaced some other word which was then in use. Whilst the Patriarchs regarded God as the faithful Promiser, Moses and his contemporaries found Him to be a faithful Performer; and in this sense they knew Him as He could not be known to their fathers. May one reflection be added? We are all children. We none of us know God fully. The wisest only knows in part.

CHAPTER XXIII.

PECULIARITIES IN BIBLICAL TERMINOLOGY.

1. The origin of language is a mystery; so is the origin *Origin of* of each particular word when neither compounded nor imita- *language.* tive. Words are the expression of ideas, and perhaps in the earliest stage of human history they were spontaneous (see Gen. **2.** 19). What really took place at Babel must have been confusion of the mind causing differentiation of speech.

We have now to do with post-Babel language only; and whilst a growing light is being thrown on its earliest forms as spoken in the region of Accad, we still know but little of the age and origin of the Hebrew of the Old Testament. It must never be forgotten that we have no Hebrew litera- ture contemporaneous with even its latest books. Conse- *Hebrew* quently we have no external means of studying the age *dialects.* and usage of any particular word except by means of the Sacred Books themselves, unless, indeed, we can find it in the inscriptions and records of Assyria, Babylon, or Egypt. Experience shows us that new words are introduced into all languages as time goes on, but they are to a large extent borrowed from neighbours; and some words which critics are inclined to call late are really provincial, if not introduced from foreign sources. Thus, in the second Psalm we have two words translated "Son," the ordinary Hebrew *Ben* (verse 7) and the Aramaic *Bar* (verse 12). It would be very hazardous to found an argument as to the date of the Psalm on the appearance of this second word. The truth is, Hebrew poetic writings affect foreign words more than prose writings do. This accounts for various words in the Song of Deborah and Barak, and elsewhere. Much has been written about the names of the musical instruments in

Daniel. It is the fashion to call them Greek, and therefore of a date later than Daniel's time, but they probably spring from Asia Minor, and can be seen in use on the bas-reliefs of Eastern potentates.

Foreign words.

2. The "ivory, apes, and peacocks" sent to king Solomon (1 Kings **10, 22**) have foreign names, possibly of Tamil origin; but who could say when they first came into being, or even when they were first used in Canaan? There are Egyptian words in the Egyptian part of the Bible, and words of Eastern origin in the Midianite part, *e.g.* the word (קבב) translated "curse" in Num. **23**, and the name of the "bracelet" in Num. **31, 50** and 2 Sam. **1, 10**. So we get Chaldean language during the period of the Captivity, and Persian words after the Return. In these and in other cases foreign words were used naturally by the writers of the time, because the circumstances and the subject-matter called for them. They thus silently bear their testimony to the veracity of the writers.

Specialities in Hebrew.

3. Many peculiar words are to be found in special portions of the Bible for the same reason. They are called for by the subject-matter. The Pentateuch, being partly legal, contains some rare, if not obsolete, law terms, which have been discussed by Michaelis in his work on *The Laws of Moses*. Being written whilst the people were on the move, it also uses "camp-language," which naturally went out of use as the people got more and more settled. We may lay it down as a rule that where circumstances are similar, similar words will be used; where circumstances are special we look for special words. In what book could "tasks" and "task-masters" be spoken of except in Exodus? or "left-handed" people except in Judges? So with "coriander" (Exodus and Numbers); and the "hornet" (Exodus, Deuteronomy, and Joshua); *Azazel* or the scapegoat (Leviticus); quarries (Judges). Other words cannot be so accounted for; *e.g.* the special word for "appointing" wages (Gen. **30, 28**), which

indicates something of the nature of a tally; and the special word for multiplication of seed, in Gen. **48**. 16, a term borrowed from the spawning of fish. In these and numerous other cases an ordinary word might easily have been used.

There are certain characteristic words generally springing out of the Pentateuch, and used consistently, if not solely, for the Deluge and the Ark, for the overthrow of Sodom, for the inundation of the Nile, for the religious warfare against the Canaanites, for casting lots, for blasphemy, for making and confirming covenants, for the proclamation of liberty, for the special visitation of blindness, for thick darkness as opposed to ordinary dusk, for being stiff-necked, &c. These words became an inheritance, and were generally used in a restricted sense.

The same is true of the numerous sacrificial, ritual, and ceremonial words which spring out of the Pentateuch. *Sacred and ceremonial words.* Many of these sacrificial words are pre-Mosaic, but they were re-issued from the mint of the great lawgiver. This class of words would include the names for the Tabernacle of the Congregation, the altar, the Ark of the Covenant, the mercy-seat, the various offerings, the technical words for " burning," which the A. V. and the R. V. so unfortunately fail to distinguish, the ephod, the Urim, the lamp, consecration, the Nazarite vow, the words for purity, sanctification, and uncleanness of different kinds. It is rarely that any of these Hebrew words are altered through the Old Testament. An exception, however, must be made in the case of the shewbread, which is described in the early books as " bread of faces," *i.e.* persons, the bread representing the person of the offerer, whilst in the Chronicles and Nehemiah the word used (מַעֲרֶכֶת) means something " set in a row," marking the orderly arrangement of the bread. It is interesting that we can here trace the growth of the new expression in the Book of Chronicles, which contains both the old term (only once, 2 Chron. **4**. 19) and the new (six times).

L

What is true of the ceremonial words of the Old Testament is true of the psychological, moral, and theological words also.*

Distinctions in Hebrew.

4. A great many of the delicate distinctions of the Hebrew are lost in the English Bible. It seems strange that three Hebrew words should be translated "window" in the account of the Flood, three translated "congregation" in Lev. 4. 14, 15, and three translated "trespass" in Lev. 5. 15. The "veil" of the Tabernacle is a very different thing from that worn by Ruth, and the "cord" of a tent is not the kind which was used to bind a man with. The king's crown was distinct from the priest's, even though an Amalekite should not be able to denote the difference (see 2 Sam. 1. 10). The "cheese" of 1 Sam. 17. 18 is not the same kind as that in 2 Sam. 17. 29; and the heart-shaped cake (queen-cake) of 2 Sam. 13 is not the same as that of 2 Sam. 6. 19, which was a sacred one. The knife used by Abraham (Gen. 22. 6) is quite a different one from that of Ezra 1. 9; if the two words had changed places critics might well have been puzzled. The word for "champion" in 1 Sam. 17. 4, 23, is not the same as that used in verse 51, and neither expression appears elsewhere, simply because it was not needed.

Agricultural words.

5. Generally speaking agricultural words are the same throughout the Bible, as would be expected; thus ploughing, reaping, threshing, are always represented by the same word; yet the sickle of Deuteronomy is not the sickle of Joel and Jeremiah (which it would have been if Deuteronomy was written in Jeremiah's time), and the word used of "old corn" in Josh. 5. 11, 12 is never used before or after. The ordinary words for flocks and herds run through the Bible, but one word translated "flocks" is only used in Deuteronomy.

---

* See *Old Testament Synonyms,* passim.

6. Commercial words are very much the same through- *Commercial*
out. Six different words are translated "merchant," the *words.*
most singular being the name Canaan or Canaanite, which
is so rendered in Job **41. 6**; Hos. **12. 7**; and Zeph. **1. 11.**
The word used for the purchase of corn in Gen. **42** and
Deut. **2. 6** is never used again for this purpose except in
Isa. **55. 1**; Amos **8. 5, 6**; and Prov. **11. 26.** The curious
thing about it is that the word itself (שֶׁבֶר) means "corn,"
which was, no doubt, one of the first objects of traffic.

7. We find a marked development of military words in *Military*
the age of David. There is a distinction in Hebrew between *words.*
an army in camp and an army in array. We find special
words growing up for companies and troops, for joining
battle, and for the trench or barricade. But there are some
special military terms in the earlier books which afterwards
become obsolete, *e.g.* the word translated "harnessed" in
Exod. **13. 18**, and "armed" in Josh. **1. 14**; **4. 13**; and
Judg. **7. 11.** The arrangement of the ranks in fives, which
the word indicates, probably died out in later years.

8. Perhaps the most interesting study of words, as bear- *Structural*
ing on the ages of the books, is to be found in what may *words.*
be called the structural language of the Old Testament.
In Exodus we have detailed provision for a movable
Sacred Tabernacle; and in Kings a permanent edifice is
set up, retaining many of the outlines and peculiarities
of the earlier structure. Exod. **25** begins with an
enumeration of various materials, including the kind of
wood to be used for all Tabernacle purposes. This is
called *Shittim* wood, being probably acacia. It is never
mentioned after the Pentateuch, though the *Shittah* tree
is once referred to amongst a group in Isa. **41. 19.** Cedar
was substituted for acacia when the Temple was built.
The *ark* is the first thing ordered to be made. It stood
unchanged through the ups and downs of Israel's history
till the Captivity. Its crown, or rim, is marked by a word
peculiar to the Pentateuch. Its lid, or mercy-seat, is only

named in the Pentateuch and in 1 Chron. **28**. 11, which
verse should be compared with the 18th, where this
sacred object is apparently described as "the chariot of
the cherubim." Next comes the *table* with its border
of a hand-breadth. It is curious that the word translated
"hand-breadth" is used of a "coping" in 1 Kings **7**. **9**.
The *candlestick*, or lamp-stand, follows in Exodus, with
its base, shaft, cups, knops, and flowers. The word for a
knop is dropped in Kings, and the "gourd" is substituted
for it. We now reach the *mishcan*, or dwelling-place of
curtains, the word being used in the Pentateuch, Joshua,
Samuel, Chronicles, and other books. The "boards," or
palings, were not wanted in Solomon's Temple, and the
word for them is only once used after the Pentateuch, viz.,
in Ezek. **27**. **6**, of the rowers' benches. The *rail* was hung
on posts (distinct from door-posts). It is only named once
after the Pentateuch, viz., in the chronicler's account of
the Temple-structure (2 Chron. **3**. 14), which is in some
respects different from that in the Kings. Directions for
the altar and the court follow. We then reach the account
of the priest's dress, containing several peculiar words.

When we turn to 1 Kings **6** we find ourselves in the thick
of mason's work, with technical builder's words never used
elsewhere. Some of the structures were carried out on the
old lines, only on a larger scale ; others, *e.g.* the porch,
having been needless before ; whilst others have almost a
foreign air about them.

The Book of Chronicles gives us both the provision made
by David (1 Chron. **28**) and the work executed under
Solomon (2 Chron. **2**, &c.). It is by no means either a
copy or a condensation of the Kings, and it contains
several peculiar words.

On reviewing the structural language in the Pentateuch,
the Kings, and the Chronicles, we have the conviction that
each narrative is in its place and in its natural order. It is
inconceivable that the Exodus narrative could be substituted
for or superseded by either of the other accounts.

CHAPTER XXIV.

THE BEARING OF TERMINOLOGY ON THE AGE OF
THE BOOKS.

1. We have pointed out that various reasons preclude us *Books grouped by their language.* from fixing the date of books by means of the appearance of particular words in them. They may have been in current use for ages before a sacred writer happened to want them, or they may have been familiar in one tribe or neighbourhood rather than in another. At the same time it is clear that the age of books may be determined to some extent, and books may be grouped, by peculiarities of language. Thus the Books of Chronicles, Ezra, Nehemiah, and Esther form a decided group, and are distinctly separate linguistically from the earlier books. Every Hebrew student would have his attention drawn to such expressions as " set office " (1 Chron. 9. 22), " clothed " (1 Chron. 15. 27), " purple " (2 Chron. 2. 7), " establishment " (2 Chron. 32. 1), " sufficiently " (2 Chron. 30. 3), " grant " (Ezra 3. 7), " interpret " (4. 7), " dram " (2. 69), " treasurer " (1. 8), " bason " (1 Chron. 28. 17), " charger and knife " (Ezra 1. 9), " copy " (4. 11), " seal " (Neh. 9. 38), " palace " (1. 1), " province " (1. 3), " letters " (2. 7), " joy " (8. 10), " children of the Captivity " (Ezra 6. 16), " appointed times " (Neh. 10. 34), &c. These are samples of many others constituting the books a distinct group.

2. There are, as a matter of fact, peculiar words in almost *Peculiar words in different ages.* every book in the Old Testament. We find them notably in Job, in each book of the Pentateuch separately, and in the Pentateuch as a whole; in Judges, Samuel, Kings, Psalms, Proverbs, and most of the Prophets; but we cannot draw an absolute line round the earlier books as we do round the latest. The terminology enables us to decide with com-

paratively little hesitation whether a book is of pre-Captivity or post-Captivity date ; but it is not so easy to decide from terminology alone whether a book is before the age of Samuel and David or after—the amount of common property in the language is so very large in proportion to the peculiarities of any particular age or person. No writer uses all the words he possesses, nor does he possess all the words that belong to his age. Hebrew was to a great extent a stationary language, and it is not easy to detect the marks of time, *i.e.* of decay and of foreign intercourse, upon it. Still, there are one or two tests which we can apply, and which may help us to decide whether the traditional view of the age of the Pentateuch and Joshua may be adhered to, or whether it must be discarded. We refer specially to the words bearing on money and measures, and also to the names of certain idolatrous objects. To these we must next call attention.

Ancient money.

3. Although we read of money transactions all through the Old Testament, we must not forget that there was no Hebrew coinage until the time of the Maccabees. To "pay" is in Hebrew to "weigh," and the Hebrew *shekel* answers to the Chaldee *tekel*, which Daniel expounded to Belshazzar. Abraham had to weigh money when he bought the cave of Machpelah, and Jeremiah had to do the same when he redeemed a piece of land, and Zechariah (11. 12) speaks of the weighing of the price at which he was

The shekel. estimated. So it comes to pass that the word "shekel" does not fix a value unless we know what the metal is which is weighed, or what is the standard of weight. The 400 shekels of silver weighed by Abraham (Gen. 23. 16) were "current" or "transferable" (עבר), whether in the form of ingots or ring-money. The golden nose-ring, or ear-ring, of Gen. 24. 22 is called a half-shekel weight. The word (בקע) here translated "half-shekel" is only found in one other place, viz., Exod. 38. 26, where we have the word itself Anglicised (*bekah*). It properly means something cleft or

divided, and is defined as " half a shekel after the shekel of
the Sanctuary." The " Sanctuary shekel " is never so
named after the Pentateuch; and we find a third of a shekel
substituted for the half in Neh. **10. 32.** We are told in
Exod. **30. 13** that the shekel contained twenty gerahs.
What, then, was a gerah ? It was evidently some small
object (? a cowry) with which Israel was acquainted in
Egypt. It is only referred to in the Pentateuch and in
Ezek. **45. 12,** which is a quotation. Another standard of
shekel is given us in 2 Sam. **14. 26,** where we read of 200
shekels " after the king's weight." This indicates that
David appointed standard weights for the country. The
word translated " weight" here is " stone," as in Lev. **19. 36,**
and in passages quoted from it. We still retain the " stone "
among our weights, and explorers have found old stone
weights in plenty in the East.

The word translated *" talent "* (כבר) first appears as a *The talent.*
weight in Exod. **25. 39.** It is used of gold, silver, brass,
iron, and lead, and is equal to 3,000 shekels, a talent of
silver being worth about 350*l.*, and of gold about 5,000*l.*
There was no opportunity for using the word in Genesis,
and we cannot fix its date, but it is a Semitic word, and may
have come from the far East with Abraham. The money
used for the purchase of Jacob's ground is called *kesitah*,
and this word is only used elsewhere in Josh. **24. 32,** which
is a quotation, and in Job **42. 11.** No one knows the real
meaning of the word, which dropped out of use in Israel,
even if retained among Arabs. The discussion on Egyptian
money transactions in Wilkinson's *Ancient Egyptians,*
chap. vii., gives interesting illustrations of the dealing with
precious metals in Patriarchal and Mosaic times.

The " dram," which is referred to in Chronicles, Ezra, and *The dram.*
Nehemiah, was thought till quite lately to get its name from
Darius, but it is now found to be older than his time. Still
it is much later than all the words which we have been
dealing with, and if we had found it in the Pentateuch or
Joshua we should at once have recognized a late hand.

Weights and measures.

4. It would be tedious to subject all the weights and measures of the Bible to a full review, but we find the same testimony throughout. Different words are introduced from different countries and at various stages of history. The *ephah*, which is a dry measure, and which is referred to frequently from Exod. **16.** 36 onwards, begins to be associated with the *bath*, a liquid measure, in 1 Kings **7.** 26, the one being probably Egyptian and the other Eastern.* The *'omer*, or handful, was a tenth of an ephah, while the *chomer*, or heap (Lev. **27.** 16, &c.), was ten ephahs, and (later) ten baths (Ezek. **45.** 14). The tenth deal of Exod. **29.** 40, &c., was probably a definite measure also. Thus a decimal system was in full swing amongst the Israelites. The cubit was a Chaldean measure, and occurs in the measurements of Noah's ark. The *cor*, and the *maneh* or pound, are Assyrian, and do not appear till the time of the Kings.

Thus the testimony of this class of words falls in with what we have found in other departments of inquiry.

Musical Instruments.

5. We might pursue the same class of investigation into the history of the musical instruments of the Bible. We have the early Chaldean harp and organ (Gen. **4.** 21), the Egyptian timbrel (Exod. **15.** 20), the ram's horn and the straight trumpet of Exodus and Numbers; then in the days of David a great development of musical instruments, including the pipe (חליל), the cymbals, the psaltery (נבל), and another stringed instrument used as an accompaniment to the song (*neginoth*) and distinct from the harp of Genesis. The absence of these Davidic and post-Davidic instruments from the earlier books is noteworthy.

Classes of idols in Old Testament.

6. The references to heathen religious and superstitions are so numerous in the Old Testament that they constitute

---

* Dr. Oppert claims the *Ap* as an Assyrian measure, and identifies it with the ephah, whilst he identifies the *imer* with the homer; but the proportions are not the same. (*Proceedings Bib. Arch.*, April 6, 1886.)

a study in themselves. No less than twelve Hebrew words are translated "idol"; some of them run more or less through the books; others are peculiar, *e.g.* the word used in 1 Kings **15**. 13. We have very scanty information about the gods whom Terah's family worshipped on the Euphrates (Josh. **24**. 2, 15), and we have to look for information on this subject to archæological discoveries in Mesopotamia. Laban's family worshipped *Teraphim* (Gen. **31**. 19, 34). These must have been of Syrian or Chaldee origin, not Egyptian, though probably akin to the little images so frequently found with mummies in Egypt.

The chapters of Leviticus and other books of the Pentateuch which warn against idolatry deal solely with Egyptian and Canaanitish rites, and not with anything Assyrian or Babylonian—a marked proof that these books are not inventions of later times. The idols of Egypt are called by a peculiar word (אֱלִיל), which perhaps means nonentity.* They are also called by a word (גִּלְגָל) which is probably intended to caricature their form, and is used in Leviticus, Deuteronomy, Kings, and Ezekiel. Canaanitish objects of worship and superstition include the *Mascith, i.e.* the bas-relief, or *intaglio*, still to be seen on the walls of the Egyptian temples as well as in Assyria, and may have been of the nature of the Hittite remains (see Lev. **26**. 1, &c.). There were also discs or sun-images (חַמָּנִים) Lev. **26**. 30), objects common to Eastern and Egyptian worship.

The *Asherah* with which the R. V. has made us familiar *The grove.* was not a grove, as the A. V. following the LXX. translated it, but a wooden image connected with Baal-worship, and probably representing the reproductive powers of Nature. It first appears in Exod. **34**. 13 in connection with the statues, pillars, or standing images of the Canaanites, and is used in the same sense all through the books.

Baal was the sun-god of Midian, Canaan, Phœnicia, and its colonies. The Hebrew form of the word (בַּעַל) means

---

* See *Old Testament Synonyms* on the various words for idols in the Bible.

master or lord, and it is usually supposed to be related to the Chaldean Bel. Baal-worship is associated with Ashtaroth-worship in Judg. **2.** 11, 13, as representing the male and female principles in Nature.

Although the plural form Ashtaroth is in the Book of Judges, the singular Ashtoreth is not found till the time of Solomon, who introduced it from Sidon (1 Kings **11.** 5, 33). It is the same as Ishtar, and is a well-known Phœnician and Babylonian deity, answering to Astarte, or Venus.

Foreign idolatry.　　Chemosh-worship was Moabite, and is referred to on the Moabite Stone (see Num. **21.** 29; Judg. **11.** 24). It was introduced by Solomon into Jerusalem (1 Kings **11.** 7). If the Levitical ordinances had been late they would have doubtless referred to it. Molech or Moloch worship was both Ammonite and Canaanite. The fire-god probably stands for the sun-god, and the abominations connected with this worship amongst the Canaanites are prohibited in Lev. **18.** 21 and **20.** 3.

Calf-worship was, of course, Egyptian, and was naturally re-introduced by Jeroboam after his sojourn in Egypt.

So far we see that the references to idolatry in the early books are of an early stamp and bear on Egyptian and Canaanitish superstitions, the Assyrian and later Babylonian worship not being referred to till the times of the Kings, and then very slightly.

Summary.　　7. A review of this discussion on Biblical terminology will tend to re-assure our minds. It is strong, cumulative, and conclusive, indicating by many instances that the books are of the age which they profess, and that they have come down in the main unchanged from the times of Moses and Samuel.

CHAPTER XXV.

POETICAL PORTIONS OF THE HISTORICAL BOOKS.

1. Although the books we have been considering are *Early prose* mainly prose, there is a strongly marked poetic element in *and poetry.* them. Indeed, in the most ancient literatures it is hard to tell where prose ends and poetry begins; there is in the one a balancing or parallelism of thought and a condensation of utterance which are the characteristic features of the other. We see this in the first recorded utterances of God and of man in the early chapters of Genesis, and notably in the words of Lamech to his wives (Gen. 4. 23, 24), which run thus :—

> Adah and Zillah, hear my voice ;
> Ye wives of Lamech, hearken unto my speech :
> For I have slain a man to my wounding,
> A young man to my hurt.
> If Cain shall be avenged sevenfold,
> Truly Lamech seventy and seven.

All proverbial sayings, if more than a few words, are semi-poetic ; see, for example, the riddle and the answer (Judg. 14. 14, 18). So it is with prophetic blessings and previsions of the destiny of nations and individuals. The first example of these predictions is to be found in the words of Noah concerning his sons (Gen. 9. 25–27) ; another early instance is the oracular answer to Rebekah concerning Esau and Jacob (Gen. 25. 23), which reads thus :—

> Two nations are in thy womb; and two peoples shall be
> parted from thy bowels :
> One people shall be stronger than the other ; and the greater
> shall serve the less.

We next meet with the celebrated benedictions bestowed by Isaac on these same sons (Gen. 27), whereby the earlier oracular response was unwittingly confirmed. The blessing of Jacob's twelve sons (Gen. 49), and the blessing of Israel by Moses (Deut. 33) are other notable instances.

Hebrew lays.

2. In all these cases the poetry is imbedded in the prose narrative, and its age and history are traditionally, if not securely, fixed thereby. The same is the case with the Songs, nine in number, which are found in the Historical Books, and which are distinctly poetic in character, as well as structure. It is natural to suppose that these Songs were dictated and written down at the time of their composition, and that many people committed them to memory. This was no hard matter in the early days of which we speak, especially in the case of the Hebrews, who are peculiarly gifted in the matter of memory. And that this was the case is shown most clearly by the fact that almost every one of these compositions is quoted in subsequent books of the Old Testament. Thus, the Song of Moses (Exod. 15), which well illustrates the normal features of Israelite poetry, is quoted in Isaiah, Micah, Nehemiah, and the Psalms; the Song of Israel (Deut. 32) is quoted in Samuel, the Kings, the Psalms, Isaiah, and Zechariah; the Song of Deborah and Barak (Judg. 5) is quoted in the Psalms; the Song of Hannah (1 Sam. 2) is quoted in the Psalms and Proverbs; the Lament of David over Saul (2 Sam. 1) is quoted in Micah; David's Song of Deliverance (2 Sam. 22) is reproduced in the Book of Psalms; David's Songs of Dedication (1 Chron. 16) are given in their expanded form in the Book of Psalms. The other two of the nine are David's last words (2 Sam. 23), and Isaiah's message to Hezekiah (2 Kings 19). With these we may associate the snatches of old poetry in Num. 21 and the utterances of Balaam in Num. 23 and 24, together with some shorter prophetic and poetic utterances which are found here and there in the Historical Books.

It must not be supposed that all prophecy is of poetic structure, or that all poetry was prophetic. The utterances of Moses concerning the Sanctuary of the Future (Deut. **12**), concerning the King (Deut. **17**), and concerning the Prophet (Deut. **18**) are quite prosaic, and in what may be called the formal legislative style. The same is true of the great prophetic chapters in Leviticus (**26**) and Deuteronomy (**28–30**), which the prophets of later days used so freely. Generally speaking, however, there was a strong association between poetry and prophecy, as can be illustrated both from the distinctively Prophetic Books and from some parts of the New Testament.

3. It is strange that some scholars, on critical grounds, *Modern critical view.* have sought to detach many of these utterances from their historical position. When we come to examine the grounds of this proposal, they appear to involve two misapprehensions. The critics have framed to themselves an artificial standard of literature, failing to recognize that poetry outstrips prose in its style and use of words.* They have also framed for themselves an artificial standard of prophecy, some of them going so far as to affirm that no prophet, however enlightened, can have uttered anything beyond the needs, or at least the experiences, of his own age. But the phenomena of literature and prophecy refuse to be bent and curtailed and fitted into any such schemes as these. We must face the facts and give credit, not only to the editors and writers of the Sacred Books, but to Him who spoke by the prophets concerning things to happen in distant ages. We are not dealing with everyday books, but with the words of men whose spiritual instincts were quickened, intensified, and enlightened by God Himself. Are there thoughts in the prophecies attributed to Moses, which no ordinary man in his times could have conceived? Why should it not be so when we read that God says concerning him, " With him

---

* See chap. xxiii., sect. 1, on this point.

will I speak mouth to mouth, even apparently, and not in
dark speeches; and the similitude of the Lord shall he
behold" (Num. **12.** 8)? Was not Deborah a prophetess?
Does anyone deny that the Spirit of God breathed in
Hannah, as in one who quoted her hymn long afterwards
(see Luke **1.** 46)? Does not David say of himself, "The
Spirit of the Lord spake by me, and his word was in my
tongue"? What do these and kindred utterances mean?
Do they not imply that the speakers and writers with whom
we have to do were lifted out of themselves, so as to become
the mouth-pieces of the Eternal, and the exponents of the
outlines of his counsels?

Ancient hea-
then poetry.

4. Modern discovery has pushed back the age of semi-
poetic language into the far distance.

When Moses was a child he might have heard the echoes of
such words as these when passing by a temple of the sun:—

> "Thou, O God, in truth art the living one,
> Standing before the two eyes.
> Thou hast created what had no existence;
> Thou hast formed all and art in all.
> We also have come into being
> Through the word of thy mouth."*

When Joseph was a youth he might have heard this ode
to the Egyptian king, Usertasen III. :—

> Hail! Khu Kau Ra, most divine of beings;
> Protecting the land of Egypt,
> Extending its boundaries;
> Whose arms reach to the nations,
> The ends of his kingdom reach up to heaven;
> The tongue of his Majesty bridles the South,
> His utterances repel the Sati;
> He is the sluice regulating the river flood,
> A refuge protecting the timorous from his foes;
> A corner that warms the shivering in winter,
> A rock that shields from the stormy tempest.†

---

* Brugsch's *Egypt*, i. 449.
† Recovered by Mr. Flinders Petrie from near the Fayum.

And when Abraham was yet young he may have heard sung to the moon-god of Ur, in Chaldæa, some such words as these :—

> Thou thy will in heaven revealest ;
> Thee celestial spirits praise ;
> Thou thy will on earth revealest ;
> Thou earth's spirits dost subdue.
> Thou through heaven and earth extendest
> Goodness, not remembering wrong.
> Lord, thy will what mortal knoweth ?
> Who with aught can it compare ?
> Lord, in heaven and earth thou rulest ;
> Of the gods none equals thee.*

If early idolaters could write such hymns as these, it would be strange indeed if their contemporaries, the enlightened agents of the true God, were to be debarred from using poetry as the medium for expressing the mind of the Eternal. Nor is there any sound reason, linguistic or otherwise, for dislodging any of the prophetic utterances referred to in this chapter from their place in the Historical Books.

---

* Tomkins' *Life of Abraham.*

CHAPTER XXVI.

NOTES ON THE SPELLING OF HEBREW WORDS.

Variations in spelling.

1. It might be thought that the age and authorship of the Hebrew Books could be tested to some degree by their orthography. We English have seen great changes of spelling during the few hundred years in which our language has been written down, and in spite of authorized or unauthorized manipulation our English Bible contains such words as vail, sope, astonied, wroth, strawed. Moreover, we find varieties of spelling in the same age. Wycliffe's name was spelt in several ways in his own lifetime, and his Bible illustrates the fact that spelling was exceedingly unsettled in his days. Even now our own Bible and Prayer Book spell words differently; thus whilst the Bible writes "judgment" the Prayer Book writes "judgement." How does the case stand in the Hebrew Bible?

Names of things.

2. The question subdivides itself according as it relates to names of places, persons, and things. To take the last first, we find but few remains of old variations such as must have existed in early times. Editors and copyists have doubtless harmonized the old spelling to a very large extent. We can indeed detect some variations in the form of words, as in the four forms of the Hebrew word for a kingdom, the three forms of the words translated garrison and ephod, the two ways of spelling the ordinary words for a village, a throne, a helmet, a pledge, parched corn, an ephah, a pit. But no argument can be founded on them, for some of the variations are not only in the same book, but even in the same chapter. The case of the word translated "helmet" illustrates this. Saul's helmet is spelt קוֹבַע and Goliath's כּוֹבַע. The difference between these is very delicate indeed,

yet it can hardly be accidental (see 1 Sam. **17.** 5 and 38);
both spellings are found in Ezekiel also. The case of the
word dram (or daric) is curious. In the first part of Ezra
(the Jeshua-narrative) it is spelt in one way; but in the last
part, which is Ezra's own narrative, the writer has added the
initial *a* (see Ezra **2.** 69 and **8.** 27). Nehemiah adopts the
former spelling, and the Chronicles the latter. There are
two spellings of the word translated "sheaf," which probably
indicate a really different pronunciation, one being pronounced *omer* and the other *amir*. The former is found
in the Pentateuch, Ruth, and Job; the latter in Amos,
Micah, and Zechariah. There is nothing, however, of real
importance so far as bearing on the history of the books
or the language.

3. Passing to the spelling of names of places, we find a *Names of*
large and perplexing study open before us. The variations *places.*
are numerous and remarkable. If we compare the old
county maps of England with the modern, we shall see
what our own local names have gone through in a hundred
years. The English Bible does not give us materials for a
complete judgment on the facts of the case as exhibited in
the Hebrew text. Thus, in Gen. **37.** 17 we read (Heb.) of
Dothain, but in 2 Kings **6.** 13, where next the place is
named, it is spelt Dothan. Some words were shortened in
the course of time. Thus Ephes-dammim (1 Sam. **17.** 1)
becomes Pas-dammim (1 Chron. **11.** 13), but then it has
the definite article prefixed. Occasionally the same place
is spelt in two ways in one chapter, *e.g.* Jabesh in Judg.
21. The case of Jericho is interesting. When it occurs in
the Pentateuch it is Jerecho; in Joshua, Jericho; in Kings,
Jerichoh; and the chronicler gives an extract from a document which retains the oldest spelling. Occasionally the
Authorized Version adds confusion, as when it gives us
Gaza and Azzah as two ways of spelling the same place.
Other changes are owing to diversities of reading, as Diphath
and Riphath in 1 Chron. **1.** 6. We can make a comparison

M

on a larger scale by comparing the Levitical cities as given in Josh. **21** with the names recorded in 1 Chron. **6.** 54–81. In this list we find Holon turned to Hilen, Ain to Ashan, Almon to Alemeth, Kishon to Kedesh, Dabarah to Daberath, Jarmuth to Ramoth, En-gannim to Anem, Helketh to Hukok, Hammoth Dor to Hamon, Kartan to Kirjathaim, &c. Many of these changes are various readings, and others are corruptions. Another list of towns is in Neh. **11.** 25–35, which may be compared with the names as given in Josh. **15** and **18**. In the first of these we find the spelling almost the same, but in the latter there are not sufficient materials for any conclusion.

It is curious in some cases to find differences between Joshua and Judges in the matter of spelling. In Judg. **1.** 30, 31, 35 we have Kitron, Nahalol, Heres, Aijelon, Shaalbim. These names stand in Josh. **19** thus: Kattah, Nahallal, Irshemesh (?), Ajalon, Shaalabbin.

The name Ephrath of Gen. **35** and **48** becomes Ephratah in Ruth. The inhabitants of Bethlehem are called Ephrathites in Ruth, **1.** 2, whilst the "Ephrathite" of 1 Sam. **1.** 1 is generally supposed to mean an Ephraimite. Some think that Joseph gave his second son the name of Ephraim in remembrance of the fact that his own mother died at Ephrath. Again, Joshua was buried at Timnath-serach (Josh. **24.** 30; compare **19.** 50). But the writer of Judges, in quoting the passage, gives it as Timnath-cheres, transposing the letters and giving the word a distinct sense, the word *cheres* being an old name for the sun, and only used in Judg. **8.** 13; **14.** 18; and Job **9.** 2. It should be noted that the word is differently spelt from that used in Isa. **19.** 18, where our translators' note should be corrected in accordance with that of the Revisers. Timneh, or Timnath, probably means a portion measured out, and *serach* would mean something remaining over and above. There is some uncertainty about the exact locality, whether Kefr-*charis*, nine miles south of Shechem, or Tibnah, west of Bethshemesh.

In Josh. **3**. 16 we read of a place called Zaretan in the
Jordan valley. This becomes Zarthan in 1 Kings **7**. 46,
and Zartanah in 1 Kings **4**. 12. The R. V. has Zaretan
throughout. It is thought by some that this is the place
called Zererath in Judg. **7**. 22, and it is certainly the same
as Zeredathah in 2 Chron. **4**. 17.

The familiar word Kirjath means city, the Phœnician
form of it (Kereth) re-appearing in the name Carthage.
The Kirjath of Josh. **14**. 15 is thought to be short for
Kirjath-jearim (Josh. **18**. 28), which is also called Kirjath-
baal or simply Baaleh.

Some of the changes, of which these are illustrations, are
simply corruptions, others had theological reasons; but we
fail to find in them any systematic changes or any tendency
which might help us to decide about the age or authorship
of the books.

4. We pass on to the consideration of the *proper names.* *Proper*
In Genesis we find the name Abram consistently used up *names.*
to a certain point, and then Abraham always. The case of
Joshua (Heb. Jehoshua) is different. He has this name in
Exod. **17**, but is called Oshea (Heb. Hoshea) in Num. **13**.
8, and the fact of his name being changed by Moses is
mentioned a few verses later. It is a pity that our translators have not represented this and some other names more
accurately. The High Priest of the Return is called Jeshua
(a later form) in Ezra **2**. 2, and so is Joshua himself in
Neh. **8**. 17; but in Zechariah and Haggai this same High
Priest is called by the true Hebrew word Jehoshua. Other
Priests and Levites with this name are referred to elsewhere,
e.g. Jeshuah (Heb. Jeshua) in 1 Chron. **24**. 11, and Jeshua
in 2 Chron. **31**. 15. We thus get a distinct tendency in the
Chronicles, Ezra, and Nehemiah to introduce the *e* sound,
while Zechariah and Haggai, the High Priest's contemporaries, stuck to the true Hebrew pronunciation and retained
the *o* sound.

The attention of critics has hardly been sufficiently directed to the fact that the name of David is systematically spelt in one way (דוד) in Samuel and Kings, and in another way (דייד) in the Chronicles. This affords a means for testing the dates and relationships of other books or passages in which the name occurs.

Origin of names.

5. Proper names are almost the only compound words in Hebrew. Every one has a meaning, and some preserve roots which would otherwise be lost, as, for example, the name Abraham. Many are historic in their origin, as Jerubbaal; others prophetic, as Noah; others theological, as Elijah, Adonijah, and Zurishaddai.

The Hebrews were fond of making a play on words, as in the case of the names of Jacob's sons. This may be illustrated from Micah and other Prophets. They were also fond of alliterations, such as Huppim and Muppim, Huz and Buz, Banni and Bunni. They sometimes changed a portion of a name; thus Uzziah becomes Azariah, and Eliakim becomes Jehoiakim, whilst Jerubbaal, Ishbaal, and Meribbaal re-appear in the forms of Jerubbesheth, Ish-bosheth, and Mephibosheth, "shame" taking the place of "Baal." It was a strange fancy to change Uriel into Zephaniah, thus turning light into darkness;* stranger still to turn Abiel into Baal, or *vice versa* (1 Sam. **14. 51**; 1 Chron. **8. 30**). Some names were twisted round. Possibly Abdon was turned into Bedan; certainly Ammiel was also called Eliam, and Ahaziah becomes Jehoahaz, Harhas becomes Hasrah, and Betah becomes Tibhath. Certain names run through endless variations. We have Shammuah, Shammoth, Shimea, Shimeah, Shimeam, Shema, Shimmah, Shimhi, all doing duty for one another.

Abbreviations.

6. Abbreviations and contractions were frequent. Thus we have Phalti-el and Phalti, Jeconiah and Coniah, Jeduthun and Ethan, Eliphelet and Eliphal, Abialbon and Abiel,

---

* Authorities, however, differ in the interpretation of this word.

Abijah and Abi, Abiezer and Jeezer. Benjamites were usually called Yaminites for a similar reason. Micah is short for Micaiah, Adoniram becomes Adoram (Kings) and Hadoram (Chronicles), Meshelemiah is called Shelemiah in the same chapter (1 Chron. **26.** 1 and 14). Many changes are apparently due to copyists, others to dialectic tendencies, others to laws of euphony. To one or other of these reasons we owe such variations as Bathshuah and Bathsheba, Merodach and Berodach, Amana and Abana, Hadad and Hadar, Dodanim and Rodanim, Jehoadah and Jarah, Amram and Hemdan, Zabdi, Zimri, and Zichri, Zabad and Zachar. There is a tendency in the later writers to substitute *i* for *u*, as Aliah for Aluah, Pai for Pau; but we find Huram in Chronicles and Hiram in Kings, being spelt Hirom in 1 Kings **7.** 40 and Hiram five verses later. The difficulty in drawing any conclusions from these is added to by the fact that writers did not adhere to one consistent spelling; thus Hazael is spelt differently in two adjoining verses (2 Kings **8.** 8, 9). Geshem the Arabian (Neh. **6.** 1), becomes Gashmu five verses later. Amnon (2 Sam. **13.** 1) becomes Aminon in the 20th verse. Nebuchadnezzar is spelt in two ways by Jeremiah; and the chronicler in the same chapter (1 Chron. **6**) gives us Adaiah and Iddo, Zophai and Zuph, Gershom and Gershon.

7. One thing is clear. No editor has attempted to harmonize the spelling. We have old materials in very old *Older and later forms.* forms. It also appears that there was a tendency in later days to soften and contract the old pronunciation; thus Araunah (Araniah) becomes Ornan; and Micaiah, Micah; and Obadiah, Abda. Again, numbers of names ending in *-jah* have in Hebrew a final *u*; *e.g.* Elijahu. There is a strong tendency in the later books to drop this last letter, as may be seen by comparing the names in Nehemiah with those in Kings. Again, there is a tendency amongst later writers to substitute a final *a* for *h*. This may be seen in

1 Chron. **1.** 9, where we have Sabta and Sabtecha for the Sabtah and Sabtechah of Genesis.

Unfortunately the Authorized Version is not accurate in little things, otherwise it would not have given Abidah in Gen. **25.** 4, and Abida in 1 Chron. **1.** 33; as also Sidon in Gen. **10.** 15, and Zidon in 1 Chron. **1**; Pharez in Gen. **38.** 29 and Perez in 1 Chron. **9.** 4; Salathiel in 1 Chron. **3.** 17 and Shealtiel in Ezra **3.** 2.

Foreign names.

8. Turning for a moment to the *foreign names* in the Bible, we find them considerably Hebraized in form and spelling, as Goim (nations) for Gutium in Gen. **14.** 1, whilst our English translations of them are Greecized or otherwise toned down. The Egyptian names Potiphar, Potipherah, Puti-el, and Phichol are fairly reproduced. Zaphnath Paaneah is much more like Egyptian in the Hebrew Bible than in the English. "So," the king of Ethiopia, is a two-syllabled word in Hebrew and in Egyptian. We have occasional variations, such as Tilgath and Tiglath, Pileser and Pilneser, which are usually indicated in the margin of the Bible. The classical form of a foreign name is often very different from the Hebrew. Ahasuerus is a better form than Xerxes, but Asnapper (Ezra **4.** 10) looks small in comparison with Sardanapalus.

Foreign gods.

No attempt was made by the Hebrews to transliterate the names of heathen gods very exactly, *e.g.* in 2 Kings **17.** 30; some may have been deliberately changed, *e.g.* Nego for Nebo in Daniel. An examination of the foreign names in the Hebrew Bible inclines us to the conclusion that they have come down in their present form from very ancient times—the Egyptian mainly from the Exodus period, and the Assyrian, Babylonian, and Persian from later ages. The evidence, indeed, is slender, but what there is confirms the view that the writings are in the main contemporary, and that they have not been manipulated to any very great extent by later writers.

CHAPTER XXVII.

NOTES ON THE STATE OF THE HEBREW TEXT.

1. Before bringing this work to a close it seems needful *Hebrew MSS.* to give some account of the state of the Hebrew text. The first printed Hebrew Bible was published at Soncino in 1488, the text being very much the same as that now found in our ordinary Hebrew Bibles. At the beginning of this century there was an examination into the age and number of the then known and accessible Hebrew MSS. by Dr. Kennicott, of Oxford, and de Rossi, of Parma. They were all European, being of Spanish, Italian, French, and German origin, and the oldest were about A.D. 1000, though some of de Rossi's fragments were two centuries older. The variations of text which were thus exhibited proved to be trivial though numerous. Other MSS. have come to light in later days, in Russia, in Damascus, in Rhodes, in Cairo, in Southern India, and even as far off as China.

Attention has been specially drawn to a MS. which exists at Aleppo, which is reported to be the actual MS. of Rabbi Aaron Ben Asher of Tiberias, to whom, in conjunction with Jacob Ben Naphtali of Babylon, we are supposed to owe our present text. This MS. is referred to by the celebrated Jewish scholar Maimonides (A.D. 1135–1204), who adopted it as his authority in the matter of accents and paragraphs. It is preserved in a cave under the synagogue. At the end of it there is a note saying that it was written by R. Solomon, a skilful scribe, and was punctuated and furnished with the Masorah by R. Aaron Ben Asher. A photograph of three columns of it is prefixed to Dr. Wickes' *Treatise on the Prose-accents* (Oxford, 1887). Dr. Wickes, however, from internal reasons, doubts if the note is trustworthy.

Their age.   2. So far as can be learnt at present there are no Hebrew MSS. older than the Christian era, unless we include some Samaritan MSS., whose claims are regarded by many critics with suspicion. What has happened to all the older Hebrew MSS.? Some may yet be brought to light, but critics have burnt their fingers by accepting fabrications, and they will be slow to acknowledge anything very ancient now. Many have been destroyed in the various persecutions which have befallen the Jews from the time of Antiochus Epiphanes onwards (1 Mac. 1. 56). It is reported that the Crusaders cut up a great many to make boots of, but this is doubtful. It is probable, however, that most have been buried, when considered to be worn out, and so they have passed away.

Variations and peculiarities in MSS.   3. All known Hebrew MSS. seem to belong to one family, and even to one section of a family. At first sight this may seem satisfactory. We have a text which is studiously followed from century to century, and which we may consider 900 years old at least. These MSS., where carefully written, are found to contain a limited number of marks, indicative of peculiarities or doubts concerning the true text. Thus there are fifteen "extraordinary points" in the Hebrew Bible. An instance will be found in Num. 21. 30 ("which reacheth unto Medeba"), where there is a point on the last letter of (אֲשֶׁר) the word translated "which," and if we remove that letter the word signifies "fire." Accordingly our Revisers have put a marginal note to that effect. (See also the LXX.) There are sixteen or eighteen "corrections of scribes," *e.g.* Gen. 18. 22, where the Hebrew now reads, "Abraham stood yet before the Lord," instead of a more ancient text in which the Lord was represented as standing before Abraham. There are five "omissions of scribes," where a single letter answering to our word "and" has been omitted as needless. There are thirteen words to be "read and not written," and five or eight to be "written and not read." There are final letters occasionally where we should expect ordinary ones, and *vice versâ*. There are large letters to indicate some peculiarities and little letters to mark others; *e.g.* in Gen. **23. 2**, where the word translated "and to weep for her," has a small letter in the middle. The reasons for these are obscure, and sometimes the Rabbis hit upon a silly one, as in the last case, where they say a small letter was introduced because Sarah was so old, and it was, therefore, unnecessary to weep much! Then there are "hanging" and "inverted" letters, such as the celebrated *n* in the word Manasseh in Judg. **18. 30**. The list of these and other peculiarities may be seen in Walton's *Preface to the Polyglot Bible*. They show us that our Hebrew Bibles really contain an *apparatus criticus* at least nine centuries old.

4. But besides these peculiarities we have a large number of various readings, which are inserted at the foot of the page in most Hebrew Bibles. It is needless for our present purpose to analyse them. Walton, quoting from Elias Levita, gives them as 848, of which only 65 are in the Pentateuch, while there are 133 in Samuel. Other critics bring the total up to 1,171. After all the number seems exceedingly small, especially as compared with the Greek Testament and its 50,000 various readings. Every precaution has been made against variations which could be made, even the letters being counted; *e.g.* there are 77,778 *m*'s in the Hebrew Bible, and 815,280 letters altogether.

Various readings.

5. But we wish to get further back. We should like to know who collected these various readings; from what sources; and why are there so many or so few? Some Jewish authorities trace the present state of things back to the age of Ezra. But this opinion is untrustworthy; for the notes are generally better than the text, and there seems no reason why Ezra should not have incorporated the best readings in the text itself. Why, for example, should the word (נערה) "damsel" be written without its last letters in about twenty passages in the Pentateuch, and be corrected

Age of variations.

throughout in the notes? Other more abstruse and mystical theories are upheld by various Jewish authorities, but none of them carry conviction.

It has been generally believed, from the days of Capellus and onwards, that we must ascribe the present condition of the text and its various readings to the Masoretic school *circa* 500 A.D., and that they secured in black and white the traditional text and the traditional variations then extant.

In Whittaker's *Historical Enquiry into the Interpretation of the Hebrew Scriptures*, published many years ago, the case is admirably treated. He concludes that the textual irregularities are not all of the same date, and the marginal corrections were not all made at the same time. The whole work was the growth of ages.

Origin of variations. 6. We must now inquire into the causes of the variations which we thus possess. Many of them are due to the fact that certain letters look very similar to one another, especially in the square character which has been used since the age of the Captivity. Thus it became very easy to put *i* (') for *u* (ו) and *d* (ד) for *r* (ר). Others are owing to the similarity of sound in words which are quite different, as in the well-known instances of *lo* (לא) "not," and *lo* (לו) "to him." Some may be caused by an old habit of not dividing words, or of spreading them out so as to fill up a line, or of abbreviating familiar words and running two letters into one. The adoption of final letters, vowels, and accents tended to reduce this class of variations to a minimum.

It is hard to know how it is that numbers vary so much, even if they were formerly expressed in letters, which is doubtful. Some ascribe the variations to deliberate corruption, but we should be slow to accept this solution.

The absence of vowel points in old times must have caused many variations. These points were not found in Paradise, as an old Jewish mystical book affirms, but gradually grew up between the second century B.C. and the fifth or sixth A.D. For a long time the Eastern and Western schools followed different systems of punctuation, but an agreement was at length attained in the tenth century A.D.

7. The word " Masorah," whence the Jewish *literati* are called " Masoretes," means tradition. All that they sought to do was to conserve the words, pauses, and sounds which had been handed down to them from old time. They collected, collated, corrected, marked the sections, divided the verses, and enlarged and systematized the vowel punctuation and accentuation. It is impossible to fix an exact date for all their work. Dr. Ginsburg considers that the initial steps were taken two or three centuries before the time of Christ, but that the whole was committed to writing at the close of the sixth century A.D., further notes of a critical character, and almost taking the place of a concordance, being accumulated up to the eleventh or twelfth century.

The Maso- rah.

8. We have by no means got to the root of our subject, however, as we desire to get further back behind the Masoretic school. There are three methods by which we can question the state of the text as it existed before and during our Lord's ministry. First, there are the quotations from the Old Testament which exist in the New. After making every deduction and accommodation possible in view of our Lord having usually spoken in Hebrew, and in view of the strong influence of the LXX. on New Testament Greek, we must conclude that the Hebrew Scriptures in current use in those days did not present the text which we now possess.

State of the text in our Lord's time.

Secondly, we have the LXX. itself. Here, again, we may make a great deal of deduction owing to the fact that readings have been corrupted, the sense has been paraphrased, double renderings have been introduced, the force of the original has been misunderstood and toned down, and glosses and traditional interpretations have been inserted. But, after all, the fact is evident that the Hebrew Scriptures current

The Septua- gint.

among the Jews of Alexandria two or three centuries B.C. were very different from those current in Palestine some centuries later.

Old Testament variations. 9. Once more, we have materials in the Old Testament itself whereby we can test the condition of things at a much earlier time. Let any one compare the second chapter of Ezra with the copy of it extracted from the archives by Nehemiah (Neh. 7. 5–73), or compare numerous historical sections, as they appear in Samuel and Kings, and as they re-appear in Chronicles. To what conclusions will the student come? He will at first feel great disappointment and dissatisfaction. He will be led to the conviction that there was not that care of the sacred text in those early days which there was afterwards. He will not only find idioms and words deliberately modernized, but letters changed, *e.g.* in proper names, and mistaken readings growing up into a new sense, hundreds turned into thousands, and numerous other omissions, additions, and variations affecting the sense. Further investigation will show him that some of these variations may not be of the nature of textual corruptions. There is method in them. We have indicated this already in the matter of proper names. The Hebrew composer had a tendency in the direction of variation where he conceived it legitimate, *i.e.* where he was not a mere copyist; and this is true, perhaps, in the case of poetry more than in that of prose. If we compare Jer. 52 with the corresponding sections in the Kings, we shall see numerous explanatory additions over and above those which are strictly supplementary or of the nature of textual corruptions; whilst in the Psalms the *Jehovah* of Judg. 5. 4, 5 is turned into *Elohim* in Ps. 68. 7, 8; the same is the case in Ps. 70 as compared with Ps. 40. 13–17, and in Ps. 53 as compared with Ps. 14, whilst other changes in these quotations are idiomatic or textual. We may illustrate this point from our modern hymnals, as many people know to their grief. We thus see three pro-

cesses at work on the text in very early days, viz., deliberate
variation, unconscious idiomatic modification, textual corruption. Moreover, we should find on full examination that
these forces were more in operation in the later than in the
earlier stages of Hebrew literature. Taken together they
will account for most of the variations in the text.

10. And so it came to pass that the Masoretic school of *Divergen-*
later days found a Hebrew text which was so imperfect that *Hebrew and*
they could easily have improved it, and yet so venerable that *LXX.*
it was only to be altered by means of the artifices enumerated
in an earlier part of this paper. How is it that this venerable text diverged so considerably from the pre-Christian
text, as exhibited in the LXX. and in the passages quoted in
the N. T. ? No critic, Jewish or Christian, seems to be
prepared with full answer; but the most probable solution
is that, while the Septuagint gives us a Western or Alexan-
drian recension, the Masoretic supplies us with the Jerusalem
text, or perhaps we should say Babylonian, for it is supposed
by ancient tradition to have been brought into its present
condition by Ezra. Which of them is likely to be the right
one? Clearly neither is faultless. We may learn from
each, and due weight must be given to the readings of each.
But special honour is due to the Jerusalem text, which
Josephus refers to as " the Scriptures laid up in the Temple "
(*Ant.* iii. 1. 7 and v. 1. 17), which Jewish translators—
Aquila, Symmachus, and Theodotion—seem to have used in
the second century A.D., and which the Masoretic school
have handed down to us as the received text.

11. A more important question now rises. Is it possible *Can we ob-*
to correct the received Hebrew text to any large extent? *tain a purer*
Probably much may be done, and the marginal readings of *text?*
our Revised Version indicate the method to be adopted,
though they are very moderate and conservative in character.
Ere many years are passed we may have (i.) a more complete collation of Hebrew MSS.; (ii.) a more trustworthy

text of the LXX.; (iii.) a re-examination of the claims of the Samaritan Scriptures, which professedly conserve a pre-Captivity text, but which agree to a large extent with the LXX.; (iv.) a more exact use of the materials preserved to us in the writings of early Christian critics, notably Origen and Jerome, together with the Syriac Old Testament and the early Jewish writings, which often supply important testimony, though it is frequently lost amid trivialities. The highest respect should be paid all the way through to the received text and its ancient various readings. There will always be numerous cases about which critics will remain in doubt. On these some light may be thrown by conjectural emendations based on the analogy of similar cases existing in the "repeated passages" in the Old Testament. Our Authorized Version does not hesitate to use these in some cases, as when it inserts the words "*and Ahaz*" into the text of 1 Chron. **9.** 41 on the strength of chap. **8.** 35, and "the brother of" in 2 Sam. **21.** 19 on the strength of 1 Chron. **20.** 5. Much more might be done in this direction, provided only that some mark were added to indicate the source of the emendation.

CHAPTER XXVIII.

1. There cannot be a doubt that a vague feeling of *Object aimed at.* disquietude has been aroused by recent inquiries into the age and compilation of the books of the Old Testament. Opinions have been advanced which tend to shake our faith in the traditional view concerning certain books, notably, those which are professedly the oldest; and the historical character of the writings, as well as the moral probity of the writers, have suffered in proportion. The foregoing pages deal chiefly with one department of the Old Testament, viz., the Historical Books. If these fall, the rest will fall with them, and the position both of Jew and of Christian will be seriously and materially affected thereby. We have attempted to present the evidence for the traditional view, and to test it by an examination of the language and contents of the book. This has been done in a series of semi-independent inquiries; and after deducting whatever is due to a natural tendency to put a case in its most favourable light, there will be found a strong cumulative argument in favour of the traditional date and order of the books being substantially the true one; and the limits of uncertainty have been proportionately reduced.

2. The course of the argument may be recapitulated thus : *Line of argument followed.* The reader was led back from the present time to the period when Jew and Christian diverged from one another; they have the same Old Testament now, therefore they must have had it then. The books were next traced back, by means of such slight evidence as was attainable, to the period of Ezra and Nehemiah, to whom tradition reasonably ascribes the

final authorization of the main body of the Hebrew Scriptures. After observing the fact that the art of writing was as old as the Patriarchs, our attention was called to the structure of the Historical Books. They evidently bear the marks of being compilations, and the materials from which they were composed are of a first-class character, being in the main from contemporary and official or prophetic sources. In order to test the integrity of the books, the quotations from the earlier Scriptures contained in the later parts of the Old Testament were examined, and it was shown that the later pre-suppose the earlier all the way up to the beginning of Genesis. The notes and parentheses in the books were next examined and classified, and they enabled us to distinguish in some measure between the writers of the original documents and the final compilers or editors of the books at each stage.

Having thus secured the antiquity and integrity of the main body of these documents—regarded as so much Hebrew literature—our next business was to consider how far they may be regarded as historical, and for this purpose we discussed the indications of the fidelity of the writers and some peculiarities in their method of composition. The internal and external tests of their trustworthiness were exhibited, and the historic character of the works was further illustrated from their chronology, genealogies, and topography.

It then became necessary to deal with two subjects which are much discussed by the critics, viz., the various stages of legislation attributed to Moses, and the use of the name Jehovah in the earliest books. This led us into an interesting but comparatively untrodden field, viz., the terminology of the Hebrew writings, and the question how far any purely linguistic tests might be devised whereby we might approximately fix the order and dates of the books.

It only then remained to point out the peculiar position which poetry holds in the prose portions of the Old Testament, and to investigate the condition of the spelling and the state of the text in the Hebrew Bible as we now have it.

3. In working out this discussion we have sought to be rational but reverential. We see no danger, but rather the contrary, in granting many things which critics demand. We must always take into consideration such possibilities as faulty translation, a degenerate text, chronological misplacement, condensations, expansions, editorial revisions, Oriental ways of expression and reckoning, combination of accounts from different sources, and such like. Thus, we allow that Genesis is a compilation, and that the writers of the original materials from which it was composed may have presented the traditional information that came into their hands in different ways, with different names for God, and from different points of view, but we believe that all these variations were Patriarchal, and that the book as we now have it is in the main as Moses and his immediate followers left it. Again, we allow that there are different codes included in the legislation of the Pentateuch, but we believe that they were all delivered to Israel through Moses in various stages of the Wilderness Wanderings, and we see no reason, literary or otherwise, for regarding any of them as fabrications of a later age. *Concessions and convictions.*

Similarly we regard the Book of Joshua as a compilation, issued in all probability under the authorization of Phinehas and the elders of his time, and we believe that it presents an authoritative account of the way and degree in which God fulfilled the promises made to the Patriarchs and to Israel. The rest of the Historical Books we take to be compilations from contemporary accounts, mainly from the works of prophetic writers, such as Samuel, the compilers themselves being persons whose authority must have been recognized when the books were issued, the final authorization of the whole being probably due to Ezra. This is the old traditional view, and to it we adhere.

N

Judging from the language and contents of the books, we see no reason for doubting, but every reason for accepting, the old view, especially if we give full recognition to the plain fact that they contain many annotations and some additions from comparatively late times, such as the days of Samuel, Hezekiah, and Ezra.

Dangers to critics. 4. We believe that many modern speculations which pass under the name of modern criticism will pass away, being proved and found wanting. We do not wish to discuss the various motives which have led some English scholars to take them up, still less do we desire to ignore the fact that there are abundant difficulties in the way of every theory, the traditional one included; we apprehend that there is a danger lest the critical school should be carried away by the current of modern materialistic and positive philosophy—that, instead of saying *omne ignotum pro magnifico*, they may be induced to say *omne ignotum pro falso*. There has been a tendency to fashion inconsistencies and discrepancies out of diversities, to bring down the date of a whole book to that of its latest utterance, to doubt the truth of a narrative if we have it in two varying accounts, to create new writers wherever new words or views are detected.

First principles of criticism. Critics are sometimes liable to forget or neglect the first principles of their art, viz., that we should give due respect to what an author says of himself, and to what his earliest followers say of him, and to what his object is, and to the spirit with which he carries it out. Many of our difficulties will be removed if we bear in mind that the books are in the main records of spiritual phenomena, that they are written in a style and language with which we have nothing parallel and contemporary, that they are not annals but extracts, being pieced together to a great extent from older materials, oral and written. It would be strange if books written at such sundry times and in such divers manners, and dealing with such ancient and often abstruse subjects, presented no difficulty to the modern student. It is evident that no attempt has been made by the Hebrew writers to remove apparent inconsistencies, which would strike the mind even of a child, *e.g.* in the chronology of the Kings, or the question of God's repentance, or the number of creatures that entered the Ark. The *Conciliator*, by Manassah-ben-Israel, translated by Lindo, gives us the Jewish interpretation of such things. Its very weakness is in its favour, and reminds us that the Hebrews were recorders, not inventors.

5. It seems very clear that some of the so-called ana- *Anachron-* chronisms (*e.g.* in Gen. **36**) are really of the nature of notes, *isms and inconsis-* and can easily be detached from the text; whilst other *tencies.* passages, which seem at first sight to be anachronisms, are sometimes capable of a simple explanation, as when the Temple of the Lord mentioned in 1 Sam. **1.** 9 proves to be the Tabernacle of the Congregation (1 Sam. **2.** 22). Others occur in prophetic utterances, and must be taken in con- nection with the predictive phenomena generally; see, for example, the references to the Lord's anointed in 1 Sam. **2.** 10 and 35. Some difficulties may have arisen through accidental misplacement or corruption of the text, as in the case of David's two introductions to Saul. Some narra- tives, which seem so like one another as to be regarded by critics as two accounts of one event, are really distinct incidents. Take, for example of this, Abraham's plan of passing Sarah off as his sister twice over, on which a German commentator has justly remarked that nothing is incredible except that the writer should have inserted both narratives unless he was certain they were true. In these and other cases critics have hardly made enough of the peculiar characteristics of Hebrew writing. They write as if they expect everything to be brought up to the critical style of the present century, regardless alike of the age of

the books, of the genius of the people, and of the spiritual intent of the writers.

Faults on both sides.

6. We freely acknowledge that those who hold the traditional view have not been free from fault. We have been afraid of allowing textual corruption, late editorial work, the use of ordinary materials, and human ways of putting things. We have confused inspiration with omniscience, and have forgotten that the treasure of Sacred Truth is committed to earthen vessels. We have minimized inconsistencies and have refused to face difficulties. We have imported modern science into ancient books, and have sought to shut up those questions about age and authorship which God in His providence has left open.

Theology and criticism.

7. Thus the merits of the case have had scant justice from both sides. But it need not be so. The critic and the theologian ought to go hand in hand. Each needs the other; each ought to respect the other. The Christian critic cannot but acknowledge that the Scriptures of the Old Testament are in some sense inspired. The writers, and in many cases the speakers, are lifted out of themselves, restrained and yet impelled, by the Spirit of God. Some special direction and help was manifestly needed if they were to give a clear account of the manifestations, purposes, covenants, and dealings of the unseen God. It was no ordinary work which they had to do, and it was no ordinary Spirit which enabled them to do it. The prophetic speakers and writers were God's pioneers preparing the way for One Who was to come, and His Spirit spoke through them and commissioned them to write.

On the other hand the writers were men, and the critical Christian must study the human side of their work. Things human and divine are interwoven throughout. We have natural phenomena and national polity and history from a Divine point of view, and we must throw all the side-lights we can on the physics and metaphysics, on the history and biography, of Scripture. We have God set forth in anthropomorphic language, and we are bound to seek and sift every human analogy by which the Hebrew writers express the Divine nature and operations.

8. The ethical convictions that accompany Biblical theology are deep and far-reaching. They made Abraham say, "Shall not the Judge of all the earth do judgment?" They made Joseph say, "How can I do this thing, and sin against God?" They made Jonathan say, "There is no restraint to the Lord to save by many or by few." They made Samuel say, "To obey is better than sacrifice, and to hearken than the fat of rams"; and again, "Man looketh on the outward appearance, but the Lord looketh on the heart." They made Solomon say, "The heaven and the heaven of heavens cannot contain Thee." These and other fundamental convictions are an inheritance to the world at large, and we owe them to the practical education which God gave to holy men of old. Is there a book in the Old Testament which may not in truth be called a theological educator? Is there one that fails in some way or other to illustrate God's way or to convey His mind? We know not any. The world would be the poorer if a single book of Scripture were allowed to perish. At the same time the critic has a right to look for a growth, a development throughout, and to investigate each section by itself in order to find out what it really contains and whence it is derived, without forgetting its relationship to the rest. In doing this, however, he must not bend facts to theories, but must be continually readjusting his theories in the light of facts. *Spiritual value of the books.*

9. The words "modern criticism" are freely used to conjure with, but the modern criticism of one age becomes ancient in the next, and we must be prepared all through *They are to be trusted.*

time for new hypotheses and new onslaughts on the old. It is so in the world of natural science, and it must be so in the realm of sacred literature. The common sense of Christian men, learned and unlearned, will stand them in good stead in the future as in the past. They will rest on the experimental argument, and will say, "God speaks to me and saves me through these books"; and that is the chief thing. They will point to the manifest honesty of the writers, and will ask convincingly whether any Jewish fabricators would have invented certain narratives concerning Noah, Abraham, Sarah, Lot, Jacob, Judah, Moses, Aaron, Miriam, Gideon, Samson, and David. They will point to the transparent candour of the historians in dealing with their own nation, of whom hardly a good word is to be found in the Scripture. If more is needed they will remind the critic of the side-lights thrown on the historic narrative all the way through, and sometimes in the most casual and incidental way, by the tablets, cylinders, and monuments of the East, and by the treasures recovered from the dust of Egypt. In a word, what main characteristic of historical and literary honesty is missing from these time-honoured documents?

The burden of discrediting the integrity of the Old Testament lies on the hostile critic. He will find it no light matter to throw overboard a large portion of the best and purest literature the world has ever seen. The task is both thankless and hopeless.

If any books bear the mark of fidelity, these do. If any are on the side of truth and rightousness, of God and Spirit, these are. They have always had enemies, but no weapon fashioned against them has prospered. Whilst some are stumbling over the literary difficulties which lie on the surface, and which may well be expected in these ancient documents, others are daily drawing encouragement and guidance from their study, for they bring the receptive reader face to face with the grandest of truths concerning God.

The difficulties which are at the bottom of much of the bewilderment of the present day largely spring from our increased sense of the magnitude and fixity of creation : the affairs of man are so small, and are under such a cast-iron rule. But if the ordinary is linked with the extra-ordinary, and the human with the superhuman, as these books testify, and if all through the ages there has been a line of Divine intervention in the affairs of man, then the mind of the student who follows the history down the centuries is prepared for some greater thing. The Old Testament points him forward, and awakens in his heart longings and expectations which are only satisfied in the Gospel of our Lord and Saviour Jesus Christ.

APPENDIX.

INDEX OF SUBJECTS.

INDEX OF TEXTS.

APPENDIX.

(*See page* 60.)

———•◦•———

Parallel Passages in Joshua and Judges.

JOSHUA 15. 15-19.

And he went up thence against the inhabitants of Debir. Now the name of Debir beforetime was Kiriath-sepher. And Caleb said, He that smiteth Kiriath-sepher, and taketh it, to him will I give Achsah my daughter to wife. And Othniel the son of Kenaz, the brother of Caleb, took it : and he gave him Achsah his daughter to wife. And it came to pass, when she came *unto him*, that she moved him to ask of her father a field : and she lighted down from off her ass ; and Caleb said unto her, What wouldest thou ? And she said, Give me a blessing ; for that thou hast set me in the land of the South, give me also springs of water. And he gave her the upper springs and the nether springs.

JUDGES 1. 11-15.

And from thence he went against the inhabitants of Debir. Now the name of Debir beforetime was Kiriath-sepher. And Caleb said, He that smiteth Kiriath-sepher, and taketh it, to him will I give Achsah my daughter to wife. And Othniel the son of Kenaz, Caleb's younger brother, took it : and he gave him Achsah his daughter to wife. And it came to pass, when she came *unto him*, that she moved him to ask of her father a field : and she lighted down from off her ass ; and Caleb said unto her, What wouldest thou ? And she said unto him, Give me a blessing ; for that thou hast set me in the land of the South, give me also springs of water. And Caleb gave her the upper springs and the nether springs.

JOSHUA 15. 63.

And as for the Jebusites, the inhabitants of Jerusalem, the children of Judah could not drive them out : but the Jebusites dwelt with the children of Judah at Jerusalem, unto this day.

JUDGES 1. 21.

And the children of Benjamin did not drive out the Jebusites that inhabited Jerusalem : but the Jebusites dwelt with the children of Benjamin in Jerusalem, unto this day.

JOSHUA 16. 10.

And they drave not out the Canaanites that dwelt in Gezer : but the Canaanites dwelt in the midst of Ephraim, unto this day, and became servants to do taskwork.

JUDGES 1. 29.

And Ephraim drave not out the Canaanites that dwelt in Gezer ; but the Canaanites dwelt in Gezer among them.

Parallel Passages in Joshua and Judges—*cont.*

JOSHUA 17. 11–13.

And Manasseh had in Issachar and in Asher Beth-shean and her towns, and Ibleam and her towns, and the inhabitants of Dor and her towns, and the inhabitants of Endor and her towns, and the inhabitants of Taanach and her towns, and the inhabitants of Megiddo and her towns, even the three heights. Yet the children of Manasseh could not drive out *the inhabitants of* those cities; but the Canaanites would dwell in that land. And it came to pass, when the children of Israel were waxen strong, that they put the Canaanites to taskwork, and did not utterly drive them out.

JUDGES 1. 27, 28.

And Manasseh did not drive out *the inhabitants of* Beth-shean and her towns, nor *of* Taanach and her towns, nor the inhabitants of Dor and her towns, nor the inhabitants of Ibleam and her towns, nor the inhabitants of Megiddo and her towns : but the Canaanites would dwell in that land. And it came to pass, when Israel was waxen strong, that they put the Canaanites to taskwork, and did not utterly drive them out.

JOSHUA 24. 28–31.

So Joshua sent the people away, every man unto his inheritance.

And it came to pass after these things, that Joshua the son of Nun, the servant of the LORD, died, being an hundred and ten years old. And they buried him in the border of his inheritance in Timnath-serah, which is in the hill country of Ephraim, on the north of the mountain of Gaash. And Israel served the LORD all the days of Joshua, and all the days of the elders that outlived Joshua, and had known all the work of the LORD, that he had wrought for Israel.

JUDGES 2. 6–9.

Now when Joshua had sent the people away, the children of Israel went every man unto his inheritance to possess the land. And the people served the LORD all the days of Joshua, and all the days of the elders that outlived Joshua, who had seen all the great work of the LORD, that he had wrought for Israel. And Joshua the son of Nun, the servant of the LORD, died, being an hundred and ten years old. And they buried him in the border of his inheritance in Timnath-heres, in the hill country of Ephraim, on the north of the mountain of Gaash.

INDEX OF SUBJECTS.

INDEX OF TEXTS.

O